Testing the CAPM,

An Unconventional Approach

Eric E. Fisher*

(May, 2017)

ABSTRACT

Previous attempts to test the CAPM using average *realized* returns as estimates of *expected* returns were not very successful nor are they likely to be. Even if the CAPM is true, any evidence of beta/return linearity that might exist in the historical record is obscured or obliterated when the average market return is near or even modestly above zero. On the other hand, estimating expected returns using average realized returns further out in the tails of the return distribution (in down markets, for example) provides evidence that strongly supports the CAPM. Using 24 years of daily return data for 90 high capitalization stocks the estimation technique developed in the paper results in expected returns that are highly correlated with beta, not just over the full 24 years, but over twelve 2-year sub-periods as well. Moreover, in a Monte Carlo experiment it is demonstrated that this alternative estimation technique delivers estimates that are closer to "true" expected returns than those resulting from the usual practice of estimating expected returns as average realizations. The robust relationship between beta and expected returns leaves little room for the so-called return anomalies to play much of a role in explaining expected returns. In particular, the statistical significance of the four non-market (*i.e.,* non-beta) return factors of the Fama/French five factor model nearly slips away entirely. In addition, with this new approach to estimating expected returns there are many fewer tangency portfolio short positions than other researchers have documented.

I. Introduction

The somewhat lofty aim of this paper is to restore the Capital Asset Pricing Model (CAPM) to its formerly preeminent position as *the* theory of equilibrium in capital markets. The plan here is to raise questions about the empirical results that have caused the theory to fall out of favor. Inevitably this requires taking a rather unconventional stance especially regarding extracting expected returns from the historical record. If it were conventional it would have been done a long time ago. But it wasn't. And it's for this reason that I've decided to publish this paper privately. I want to get the

---

* Formerly Senior Managing Director of Quantitative Portfolio Management and Trading at TIAA-CREF, Retired in 2000.

Note: Permission granted to copy. Also available from Amazon in hard copy and on Kindle.

idea out there where it can be critiqued on its merits (or their lack) and not quashed because it is, well, unconventional.

Building on the work of Harry Markowitz's "Portfolio Selection" (1952) and the Separation Theorem of James Tobin (1958), the CAPM was originally developed[1] by William Sharpe (1964) and John Linter (1965). For many years the model reigned supreme. But nowadays the common view is that the CAPM is somewhat of an enigma. On the theoretical side, things seem to be in pretty good shape. In his excellent book: The Capital Asset Pricing Model in the 21st Century," for example, Haim Levy (2012) observes " … the CAPM has turned out to be one of the pillars of finance and economics of uncertainty and asset pricing." It's on the empirical side where things get messy. Indeed for many decades using and testing the theory has confounded practitioners and academics alike.

Practitioners have tried to find mispriced securities by comparing the theory's equilibrium expected returns against their own privately held expected returns derived typically from a dividend discount model. But their efforts were not rewarded with much success.

Academics have tried to find empirical evidence that strongly supports this *ex ante* theory of equilibrium in capital markets by looking at various *ex post* statistics with disappointing results. Early cross-sectional regression tests of average realized returns as estimates of expected returns on time-series regression estimates of betas seemed to support the Sharpe-Lintner CAPM but ultimately rejected it. The intercept was too high (far from any reasonable proxy for a "riskless" rate) and the slope too low – both very different from what was predicted by the model. The less restrictive Fischer Black (1972) "zero-beta" version of the CAPM based on unrestricted short selling and without a riskless rate fared better until it was noticed that other variables most notably market capitalization (Banz, 1981) and book-to-price (Rosenberg, Reid, Lanstein, 1985) played an important role in explaining average realized returns. With the discovery of these "anomalies," the CAPM appeared to be in serious trouble (another case of a beautiful theory seemingly "killed by an ugly fact"[2]) and the explanation of equilibrium in capital markets took on a decidedly empirical tone. Market capitalization and book-to-price (as well as beta) became incorporated into the well-known Fama and French (1993) three factor model for stocks. Although both authors bemoaned the excessively empirical nature of their model, the lure of finally explaining average realized returns was sufficiently strong that their 3-factor model morphed into the Fama and French (2014) 5-factor model. Two more factors were added: one related to investments and the other to profitability. All of these factors – these anomalous facts – and the literature is replete with many more – contributed to a gnawing sense that the CAPM was dying[3], but they didn't deliver that fatal blow for the simple reason that there is no theory to suggest that these anomalies (they are after all *anomalies*) matter at all. They could go away. "In economics it takes a theory to kill a theory; facts can only dent the theorist's hide" (Samuelson, 1951).

But with the publication of Richard Roll's "A Critique of the Asset Pricing Theory's Tests" in 1977, it became clear that the CAPM was in trouble even before many of the anomalies were

---

[1] Jack Treynor (1962) wrote a version of the CAPM and circulated a "mimeographed" copy in the fall of 1962. Unfortunately it wasn't available in a published form until 1999. Had he published it in the early 60's, it's generally conceded that he would have shared the 1990 Nobel Memorial Prize in Economic Sciences along with William Sharpe and Harry Markowitz. Somewhat later Jan Mossin (1966) developed and published another version of the CAPM.

[2] Attributed to Thomas H. Huxley (1825-1895)

[3] Indeed many have declared it already dead. Pettengill, Chang and Hueng (2012) identify two regimes in the literature: the CAPM regime "dated from the Mid 1960s through the early 1990s, and the Fama-French three-factor model (FF-3FM) regime, which may be dated from the early 1990s to the present day."

discovered. The most widely cited major point in the paper, *viz.*: that since the market portfolio is assumed to contain everything that could have a price, it's unobservable. Real world market indices invariably fall short of this ideal because it's hard, if not impossible, to get a price for things like human capital, stamp collections, jewelry, antique cars, even real estate, etc. that should be in the market portfolio along with easily priced assets like stocks and bonds. On the face of it, this failure is not too much different from the failure to find that expectations are homogeneous (a major, crucial assumption of the CAPM). Neither should dissuade us, however, from accumulating evidence that might persuade reasonable people to assume that market participants act "as if" (as Milton Friedman explains in his 1953 influential essay, "The Methodology of Positive Economics"[4]) the major unrealistic assumptions of a theory were true. In the case of the CAPM, we're being asked to assume that expectations are all more or less the same for everyone and that stock market indices are reasonable proxies for the elusive, all inclusive "market portfolio."[5] The key, and this is a major point that Friedman stresses, is that a theory, however unrealistic its assumptions or implications, must result in good predictions. With the CAPM the major prediction is that there is only one factor (*i.e.*, the market) that explains *expected* returns. As will be shown, when expected excess returns are measured in a particular way this is indeed the case, as many of the "anomalous" factor returns descend into statistical insignificance.

In what follows, the demonstration of this fact relies heavily on empirically showing a strong linear relationship between expected return and beta. But use of this relationship, even if very strong, has been roundly criticize by Roll (1977) and Roll and Ross (1985). In their view, getting a close relationship just isn't good enough. It's got to be exact. "The cross-sectional relation between expected return and beta, whether it is exact, imperfect, or zero, is completely determined by the position of the index." (Roll and Ross (1994), p. 102). They have argued that if the index used to estimate beta is not efficient, betas are not reliable because another inefficient index could be found that turned a positive relationship into a negative one. Grauer (1999) notes, however, that this observation applies "in universes where all assets are observed ..." (p.788). And this is the case in this study where only a limited number of assets (just 90 stocks) are used. Furthermore, it's unclear, to me at least, that this sort of reversal doesn't depend on the existence in the index of short positions and/or excessive weight of a few stocks and in the variance matrix on a number of negative or zero covariances among stocks. But even if none of these conditions were present, we could still argue, along with Levy and Roll (2010) that with a bit of tweaking of the input parameters "the market portfolio may be mean-variance efficient after all." And if it is efficient, what better way to demonstrate the predictability of the CAPM than with a strong empirical expected return/beta linear

---

[4] See, Friedman, Milton. 1953. "The Methodology of Positive Economics," reprinted in Hausman (2008) University of Chicago Press.

[5] We could take a different tack entirely: Empirical evidence seems to support the adoption of a non-theoretical asset pricing model such as the Fama/French 5 factor model. But since that same empirical evidence (handled differently, as we shall see below) makes an even stronger case for *beta alone* explaining estimated expected excess returns, doesn't it make sense to embrace the simpler model – something like the market model with expectations (albeit estimated) in place of average realizations? This would be tantamount to accepting a one factor APT model (Ross (1976)) with its less restrictive assumption (*i.e.*, the index, as a factor, need not be efficient and less than perfect return/beta linearity is acceptable as a way of demonstrating how beta truly does explain estimated expected excess returns, etc.). But then, just like others, we'd be stuck with a strong empirical model in search of a theory. Better, I think, to stick with the theory we have in spite of all its problems. In other words start with the Arbitrage Pricing Model, empirically demonstrate the dominance of a single factor of estimated expected return, dust off CAPM and announce, "We knew that was the case all along." Market portfolio efficiency (along with perfect return/beta linearity) exists in the CAPM ideal, but we should never see it perfectly played out in reality, nor would we want to. Because if it were, we'd end up hopelessly baffled by the extent and level of trading that actually does take place.

relationship, since in the theory (albeit freighted with unreasonable assumptions) linearity necessarily follows from efficiency and the other way around (proof in Appendix A).

II. Testing the CAPM

Most tests of the CAPM using stocks, used *average* realized returns as if they were *expected* returns. This is certainly true in the early well-known tests of Black, Jensen, and Scholes (1972); and Fama and MacBeth (1973). It is also true in the later Gibbon, Ross, Shanken (1989) more fundamental test of the efficiency of the market portfolio. Even the more recent Levy and Roll (2010) procedure which altered the sample parameters of both the variance matrix and the return vector to allow for sampling error used average realized returns over a particular time period and concluded, as already noted and as the title of their paper states: "The Market Portfolio May Be Mean-Variance Efficient After All."

The justification for testing an expectational model in terms of realizations seems to be based on the notion as Elton, Gruber, Brown and Goetzmann (2014, p. 331) note, "… that expectations are on average and, on the whole, correct. Therefore over long periods of time, actual events can be taken as proxies for expectations." Although reasonable the assumption that realized returns are decent estimates of expected returns has been questioned over the years. It was famously questioned by Edwin Elton himself (1999) in his American Finance Association presidential address. No doubt it should have been vigorously questioned sooner if for no other reason than that realized excess returns (returns minus the risk-free rate) are often negative even for long periods of time (Elton cites the 11 year period from 1973 to 1984 when average realized stock market returns were less than the risk-free rate).[6] Clearly a negative average realized excess return could not possibly be a proxy for an *expected* excess return. In a speculative market, widely held expected excess returns can't be negative (or, can't be negative for long). Just as clearly, this is a problem that extends beyond periods where average realized excess returns are negative or zero. It exists even when market excess returns are modestly positive, which is usually the case over extended periods.

To demonstrate this last point, imagine a very simple return generating process where individual stock excess returns, $r_{i,t}$, are generated by a sensitivity, β_i, to the market excess return, $r_{m,t}$, plus an idiosyncratic return, α_i, which doesn't last long, plus noise, $\epsilon_{i,t}$, (assumed here to have a mean of zero, even for small or smallish samples). In other words, assume that something like the CAPM is the case (*i.e.*, that alphas exist now and then) and that the single factor that explains expected excess returns, β, also explains realized excess returns:

$$r_{i,t} = \alpha_i + \beta_i r_{m,t} + \epsilon_{i,t}. \tag{1}$$

Averaging over a sample time period gives:

$$\overline{r_i} = \alpha_i + \beta_i \overline{r_m}. \tag{2}$$

Then, assuming that alphas and betas vary from stock to stock, the sample variance of average realized excess returns *across* stocks is:

---

[6] To which I can add the nearly 16 year period from the local peak at 9/3/29 to the local trough at 8/24/45 when the stock market (CRSP index) was similarly below the Treasury bill rate.

$$\hat{\sigma}_{\bar{r}}^2 = \hat{\sigma}_{\alpha}^2 + \bar{r}_m^2 \hat{\sigma}_{\beta}^2 + 2\bar{r}_m \widehat{Cov}(\alpha,\beta). \quad (3)$$

And the coefficient of determination between average realized excess return and beta is:

$$R^2_{\bar{r} \, vs.\beta} = \frac{\widehat{Cov}(\bar{r},\beta)^2}{\hat{\sigma}_{\bar{r}}^2 \hat{\sigma}_{\beta}^2} = \frac{\widehat{Cov}(\alpha,\beta)^2 + \bar{r}_m^2 \hat{\sigma}_{\beta}^4 + 2\bar{r}_m \hat{\sigma}_{\beta}^2 \widehat{Cov}(\alpha,\beta)}{\hat{\sigma}_{\alpha}^2 \hat{\sigma}_{\beta}^2 + \bar{r}_m^2 \hat{\sigma}_{\beta}^4 + 2\bar{r}_m \hat{\sigma}_{\beta}^2 \widehat{Cov}(\alpha,\beta)}. \quad (4)$$

Equation (4) is a bit messy. If we assume there is no correlation between the alphas and betas across stocks (*i.e.*, if $cov(\alpha,\beta)=0$), as there shouldn't be,[7] then the coefficient of determination between average realized excess return and beta is simpler:

$$R^2_{\bar{r} \, vs.\beta} = \frac{\widehat{Cov}(\beta \bar{r}_m + \bar{\alpha}, \beta)^2}{[\bar{r}_m^2 \hat{\sigma}_{\beta}^2 + \hat{\sigma}_{\alpha}^2]\hat{\sigma}_{\beta}^2} = \frac{\bar{r}_m^2 \hat{\sigma}_{\beta}^4}{\bar{r}_m^2 \hat{\sigma}_{\beta}^4 + \hat{\sigma}_{\alpha}^2 \hat{\sigma}_{\beta}^2}$$

or,
$$R^2_{\bar{r} \, vs.\beta} = 1/[1 + \left(\frac{1}{\bar{r}_m^2}\right)\left(\frac{\hat{\sigma}_{\alpha}^2}{\hat{\sigma}_{\beta}^2}\right)]. \quad (5)$$

Obviously if the average market excess return is near zero, then the R^2 between average excess returns and beta is near zero as well. This makes sense; if the market is flat over some long period then average excess returns differ from one another in a way that has nothing to do with beta even though beta is driving them (if the model given by equation (1) is true) over shorter periods. What variation they do display is due to their alphas. Thus, even if the CAPM is true as we've hypothesized and even if realizations are in line with expectations as we've surmised, only when the market is strongly positive or negative do we stand a chance of proving the CAPM; *i.e.*, of differentiating the excess returns of stocks on the basis of their sensitivity to the market factor.[8]

It would seem, therefore, that in order to demonstrate the validity of the CAPM using average realizations in place of expectations (or rather, as *estimates* of expectations), we have to *pick* a particular sample. But picking a particular sample means that it's not a *random* sample, which violates everything we know about hypothesis testing. And lest one thinks that if the sample were only long enough to let expected returns stand out, one need only be reminded of Elton's observation above.

What's needed is a way to test the CAPM with *any* sample and over *any* time period. But before turning to a way to do that, it's useful for the subsequent tests to view the CAPM in a slightly different light.

---

[7] In other words, high (low) beta stocks don't always have high (low) alphas and the other way around. But obviously in any sample, the estimated covariance, $\widehat{Cov}(\alpha,\beta)$, could easily be non-zero, especially if the time period is short. Turns out that this is indeed the case for 12 two year sub periods using daily data (see the discussion on page 12). Over longer periods it's difficult to supply a reason why the covariance should be anything other than zero. And over 24 years of daily data, as we shall see, it isn't.

[8] Note if all the alphas are zero, then so is $\widehat{Var}(\alpha)$, and we end up with perfect correlation (market portfolio demonstrably efficient). This topic is visited more thoroughly below.

III. CAPM as a Platonic Form

The CAPM is timeless The theory simply describes what an equilibrium would look like, not how long it would take to achieve it, or indeed if it would take any time at all. Equilibrium abstracted from the process that creates it is clearly an idealization not unlike the notion of a Platonic Form or Idea that transcends time on a par with, for example, "timeless" equilibrium price determination for goods and services as the intersection of demand and supply schedules. Like other timeless equilibrium theories in economics, the CAPM is true (see proof in Appendix A). Its conclusions necessarily follow from its assumptions. The issue for testing the CPM is whether real world capital market equilibria which take place in time partake of the CAPM ideal (are instantiations of "CAPMness" if you will). And by instantiation we can't mean a perfect match in the same way we can't mean that any experienced thing, any horse, for example, is a perfect match for the Platonic Form: horseness. All horses are imperfect instantiations of horseness as are all instantiations of CAPMness in this view. Knowing this, we can't get too exercised when we're unable to demonstrate that the market portfolio is exactly *ex-post* mean-variance efficient, or that there is a perfect linear relationship between beta (calculated from a sample which is an *estimate* of the real thing) and realized average excess return (which is an *estimate* of the true expected excess return). We do need to get close though. In the case of return/beta linearity we do need to find a high R^2.

A big advantage to formally untethering the inputs to the CAPM from time, is that it becomes unnecessary to assume that all investors have the same holding period, or any holding period at all. From this point-of-view expected returns can be taken simply as abstract characteristics. And risk can be view similarly. The abstract character of both is manifestly evident in the proof of the CAPM laid out in Appendix A. There, it is just symbols that are being manipulated in an environment where there are a few rules and, importantly, no time. The trouble begins when we interpret the symbols and feel the need to supply a narrative that includes things like a common holding period. Indeed CAPM could be viewed somewhat fancifully as an activity where robots put together collections of finitely divisible objects each of which has two characteristics: a variable good one and a fixed bad one and where they are programmed to minimize the collection's overall bad characteristic at a given level of the good characteristic. With 1) some rules about how these objects combine in the collections, 2) the existence of a "bad-less" object, and 3) different programmed levels of "bad" aversion in each robot, it follows from Tobin's Separation Theorem (1958) that these robots all put together the same collection of objects (the "tangency collection," if you will). And from there, with the additional assumption that all object are collected, it's just a few steps to the CAPM-like conclusion that the level of good in an object is a function of the level of good in the "bad-less" object plus a sensitivity to the level of good in the tangency collection in excess of the good in the "bad-less" object.

Of course the story should be fleshed out a bit more (especially as regards what the tangency collection is tangent to) but to go on and on could get, if it hasn't already, rather tedious. Perhaps the point has been made. Whether couched abstractly, fancifully, or in the terms with which we are all familiar, the CAPM ends up with a statement about what expected returns are (or, have to be) even though it seems that the whole process started with them in the first place. What they have to be is a *linearly function* of beta times the true market portfolio's expected return, $E(R_{mkt})$, where beta is calculated relative to the true market portfolio itself (See equation (A11) in Appendix A):

$$E(R_i) = r_f + \beta_{i,mkt}[E(R_{mkt}) - r_f]), \quad \text{where } \beta_{i,mkt} = \frac{Cov(R,R_{mkt})}{Var(R_{mkt})}$$

This is the theory. This is the Platonic Form. Note that although I carelessly said we start off with expected returns and end up with them having to be a certain way. There's nothing about a process here (like an iterative one that converges). There can't be. Time doesn't exist in the CAPM. The CAPM just is. This is the way it all hangs together. The CAPM simply shows us what equilibrium looks like – not how we got there.

But instantiations of this CAPM Platonic Form in the real world do involve time. In my view the trick in terms of testing the CAPM is to look beyond our need always to view time as an ordered sequence and instead separate out and look at the "times" when the pattern we hope to discover (the tune we hope to hear, as it were) is less distorted by other patterns and/or by just noise.

IV. A Different Method of Estimating Expected Excess Returns

The CAPM is consistent with any return generating process for the simple reason that the theory says nothing about how actual returns are generated.[9] The theory is about future returns and what they are expected to be, not about what they have been. However, in forming expected returns investors can't avoid the past. They have to have some idea of how returns were generated in the past to guess how they might be generated in the future. And if this informs their expectations and they act on it, then the returns that are realized in the market will contain a trace, and hopefully a very good one, of what the expectations were.

To get at a return generating process that might lead to a way to estimate expected excess returns (again, returns minus the risk free rate), let's start by assuming that a CAPM equilibrium exists every day:

$$E(r_{i,t}) = E(\beta_{i,t} r_{m,t}) \tag{7}$$

where $r_{i,t}$ is an individual stock's excess returns and $r_{m,t}$ is the excess return of the market portfolio. And let's not make any assumptions for the moment about the stability of the variance matrix and hence of beta which is why it has a time (day) subscript attached to it. It's allowed to vary over time (to change every day), just as $E(r_{m,t})$ is allowed to vary which of course means that the $E(r_{i,t})$s are allowed to vary as well.

Now, if, as seems reasonable, the covariance between beta and the excess return of the market is zero (i.e., $Cov(\beta_{i,t}, r_{m,t}) = 0$), then we can rewrite (7) as:

$$E(r_{i,t}) = E(\beta_{i,t})E(r_{m,t}), \tag{8}$$

since $Cov(\beta_{i,t}, r_{m,t}) \equiv E(\beta_{i,t} r_{m,t}) - E(\beta_{i,t})E(r_{m,t})$.

Then, replacing the expectations in equation (8) with sample averages, and substituting an excess return of a stock market index, $r_{index,t}$, for the excess return of the unobservable market portfolio, $r_{m,t}$, we get:

---

[9] See Sharpe's Nobel Lecture (1990)

$$\overline{r_i} = \overline{\beta_i}\,\overline{r}_{index}. \tag{9}$$

What equation (9) says is that if every day a theoretical CAPM equilibrium exists (i.e., if the CAPM is true), then in *any* sample over *any* number of days no matter how many or few, there should be a perfect relationship between *average* beta and *average* realized excess return across all stocks. And, importantly, since the CAPM is timeless, the days need not be consecutive. They can be any days. They can be days when there's a full moon, or when there's sun spots, or when the market makes a positive or negative move. In other words, if the CAPM is true, Equation (9) specifies a return generating process that holds even if beta changes. This is because if beta changes, so does expected excess return and the average linear return/beta relationship remains intact.

Now insofar as the sensitivity of a stock's return to the market's return as measured by beta is based on a company's capital structure, product line, industry, etc. and these things don't change overnight, we can expect beta to be somewhat stable over time as well. If beta changes it probably does so slowly along with the slow evolution of company characteristics. Thus when we come to measure beta we should be able to include days when the phenomenon we're investigating is *not* occurring just so long as those days are near those when it is. For example, if we're interested in the linear relationship between beta and realized excess return when the market is making a negative move, say, including days when the market is positive for the purpose of measuring beta is acceptable as long as those positive days are not separated from the negative days by a lot of time. The advantage is that as we make the sample size bigger, statistical reliability improves.

The timeless nature of the CAPM allows us to fracture the ordered nature of time and form pseudo portfolios designed to let what we're trying to measure shine through. The motivation here is similar to what I imagine is behind the Fama-French (1993) procedure of forming special portfolios which exaggerate the characteristic being studied (high beta vs low beta, high book-to-price vs. low book-to-price, large cap vs. small cap, etc). They formed realistic portfolios of stocks and measured performance over all time periods, here I am proposing forming pseudo portfolios for each stock and measuring average performance for all the days when the market's excess return is positive in one pseudo portfolio and negative in another. The idea here is to look at realized excess returns in a way that avoids the problems documented in equations (4) and (5). Of course we expect each stock's average excess returns for days when the market is negative to be negative, and when it is positive to be positive. Even a casual observer cannot help but notice that when the market goes up most stocks go up and the opposite when the market goes down. Although obvious to the point of tautology (when most stocks go up, most stocks go up, and so on), what I'm looking for here is an answer to the question: *when the market's negative, does beta separate out big losers from not so big losers and when the market's positive, big winners from moderate winners?*

Unfortunately with this approach we end up with a big negative average excess return for the negative-days-pseudo portfolio and a big positive number for the positive-days-pseudo portfolio. By themselves they can't be compared to anything. They don't' find a place alongside other rates of change in value like saving account interest rates, long term equity returns, bond yield-to-maturities, etc.. We want to come up with a *single* expected excess return for each stock that looks like other expected excess returns. Obviously we can't just form a weighted average of these two average excess returns because we'd end up right back with the regular overall average excess return and its problems.

What's needed is a way to scale the negative and positive averages so they're comparable not just to each other but to the overall average of all days (both positive and negative). Making each pseudo portfolio's average excess return relative to the average of all stocks for the same days accomplishes this. For example, a negative average excess return for a stock's negative-days-pseudo portfolio gets divided by the average excess return for all stock's negative-days-pseudo portfolios, typically resulting in a positive *relative* average excess return even though it's for negative days. Since these relatives are normalized (they average 1), they can be multiplied by any estimate of the expected excess return for stocks to get a series of expected excess returns that have a familiar scale. For this study, they are multiplied by the average realized excess return for all stocks (as measured by the "CRSP Index," see below) over the period under consideration.

Finally, since these two relative estimates come from the same overall time period, they're combined into a single weighted average where the weights are proportional to the number of days applied to each pseudo portfolio. The justification for combining positive and negative average excess returns is based on equation (9) which does not distinguish between positive and negative days. For each stock, all the days when the market is negative are gathered up, averaged and divided by the overall average of these averages on negative days to get the relative: $\bar{r}_i^- / (\sum_j^k \bar{r}_j^- / k)$ (where k = number of stocks). The same is done for positive days to get: $\bar{r}_i^+ / (\sum_j^k \bar{r}_j^+ / k)$. If the CAPM is true, we know from equation (9) that a weighted average of these two relatives should equal the average beta, $\overline{\beta_i}$ for all days (positive and negative).[10]

To summarize, what we have is a weighted average of normalized positive and negative average daily realized excess returns relative to all stock's positive and negative average daily realized excess returns scaled so that their mean is the same as the mean of average realized excess returns. Clearly a mouthful, so let's just refer to them as the "**PAN AERs**" for **P**ositive **A**nd **N**egative **A**verage **E**xcess **R**eturn**s**. And let's refer to **A**verage **E**xcess **R**eturn**s** as simply "**AERs**."

The mechanics of how everything is put together for **PAN AERs** is best displayed as a formula:

$$\textbf{PAN AER}_i = \bar{r}_{CRSP} \left[\lambda \left(\frac{\bar{r}_i^-}{\sum_j^k \bar{r}_j^- / k} \right) + (1 - \lambda) \left(\frac{\bar{r}_i^+}{\sum_j^k \bar{r}_j^+ / k} \right) \right] \quad (10)$$

where: $\bar{r}_i^- = \bar{r}_i \big| (t)(r_{mkt,t} \leq 0)$ [11] and similarly for $\bar{r}_i^+$, *mutatis mutandis*.

λ = number of negative days divided by total number of days
k = number of stocks (=90)
$\bar{r}_{CRSP}$ = Average daily excess return for the CRSP index

---

[10] $\overline{\beta_i}$ here is estimated as the OLS slope in a regression of $r_{i,t}$ on $r_{index,t}$. Of course, technically this OLS slope is not an average at all. What we're after here is the average of *single day* betas. But with daily data we can't observe a single day's beta. We need many more observations. We can, however, see if the beta for a long period is close to the average of shorter period betas. With 24 years of daily data for 90 stocks (a description of which is in section V on page 10) I calculated betas for each stock for 250 days (approximately one year) and compared the average of these 24 betas to the beta calculated over the entire period (6,046 observations). The coefficient of determination for these 90 observations of the average slope versus the overall slope was .92. This jumped to .98 if 1% of the most extreme positive and 1% of the most negative observations are eliminated as described in section VIII on page 19. Approximating an average of short term betas with a long term beta appears to be justified.

[11] Read " $\bar{r}_i \big| (t)(r_{mkt,t} \leq 0)$ " as the average excess return for the ith stock given all the times (t) that the market excess return is less than or equal to zero.

V. The Data

Anyone testing the CAPM must select a surrogate market portfolio to stand in for the true, unobservable, market portfolio. Common practice, which I follow here, is to select an equity index of the U.S. stock market. It's obviously not *the* market portfolio, not even close, because it doesn't contain things like human capital, or even bonds and it's only for the U.S.. But it *is* broadly based. And it is my contention that if it can be demonstrated that it *close* to the tangency portfolio (the point on the minimum variance frontier that is tangent to a line up from the risk-free rate in return/standard deviation space) then we can conclude that investors behave "as if" (Friedman's positive economics again) it is indeed the market portfolio and that it *is* mean-variance efficient[12]

For the tests that follow I've selected a portfolio consisting of a value-weighting of the daily common stock returns of all CRSP firms incorporated in the US (hereafter and previously referred to as the "CRSP Index") Daily returns for this index along with the Fama/French 5 factors as well as Treasury bill rates (from Ibbotson Associates), were all downloaded from the Kenneth R. French (2016) Data Library in July, 2016.

Next, because I believed it is important to see if the percentage of tangency portfolio weights (the calculation of which involved taking the inverse of the sample variance matrix) is near 50% as shown to be the case by Levy and Ritov (2011) I wanted to avoid a large sample. Somewhat arbitrarily, the same 100 largest US stocks (as of 12/31/2010) that were used in a working paper by Brière, Drut, Migno, Oosterlinck, and Szafarz (2011) were selected. Use of a dataset selected in the past has the advantage of avoiding survivor bias from the selection date to the present (six years or so in this case). It turns out that for one reason or another I only ended up with the largest 90 stocks (see Appendix C). Daily closing prices adjusted for stock splits, stock dividends and cash dividends for these 90 stocks were downloaded from the YAHOO financial database (also in July, 2016) for the 24 years from 5/29/1992 to 5/31/2016, giving a total of 6,046 observations.[13] Daily excess returns were then calculated as the adjusted percent price change minus the Treasury bill rate. The expected excess return variance matrix was simply estimated by the 90X90 matrix of sample variances and covariance (hereafter the "sample variance matrix" or just "variance matrix").

There is nothing very new in all of this so far, except perhaps the use of daily data. The reader will appreciate however, that the cards are somewhat stacked against the tests that follow if for no other reason than with daily data closing prices sometimes merely bounce between bids and offers creating noise and obscuring any signal that might be present. Moreover tests are not on the zero-beta Black model (1972), but on the more restrictive original Sharpe-Lintner model where the existence of a riskless rate is assumed.

What is new, however, is that expected excess returns are estimated not as **AERs** over all market conditions (the baseline case, investigated in the next section) but as **PAN AERs** (the superiority of which is investigated starting in Section VII).

---

[12] Mean-variance efficiency is a relative attribute. A portfolio is not designated mean-variance efficient and that's the end of it. It's only mean-variance efficient relative to a specific collection of expected returns and a variance matrix. A portfolio that is mean-variance efficient relative to one collection of expected returns, for example, probably is not mean-variance efficient relative to another collection even though they might share the same variance matrix.

[13] Use of CRSP data would have been preferable. But since I'm retired, I no longer have an institutional affiliation.

VI. Baseline: Beta vs. AERs (as Estimates of Expected Excess Returns)

Previous researchers have looked at average realized excess returns relative to beta, and found, as Fama and French (2004) noted, that the relation is "too flat" and that "…the intercept is greater than the average risk-free rate (typically proxied as the return on a one-month Treasury bill)." For the data at hand, for the entire 24 year period, with betas calculated relative to the CRSP index the relationship is shown in Figure 1 (standard errors are in parenthesis):

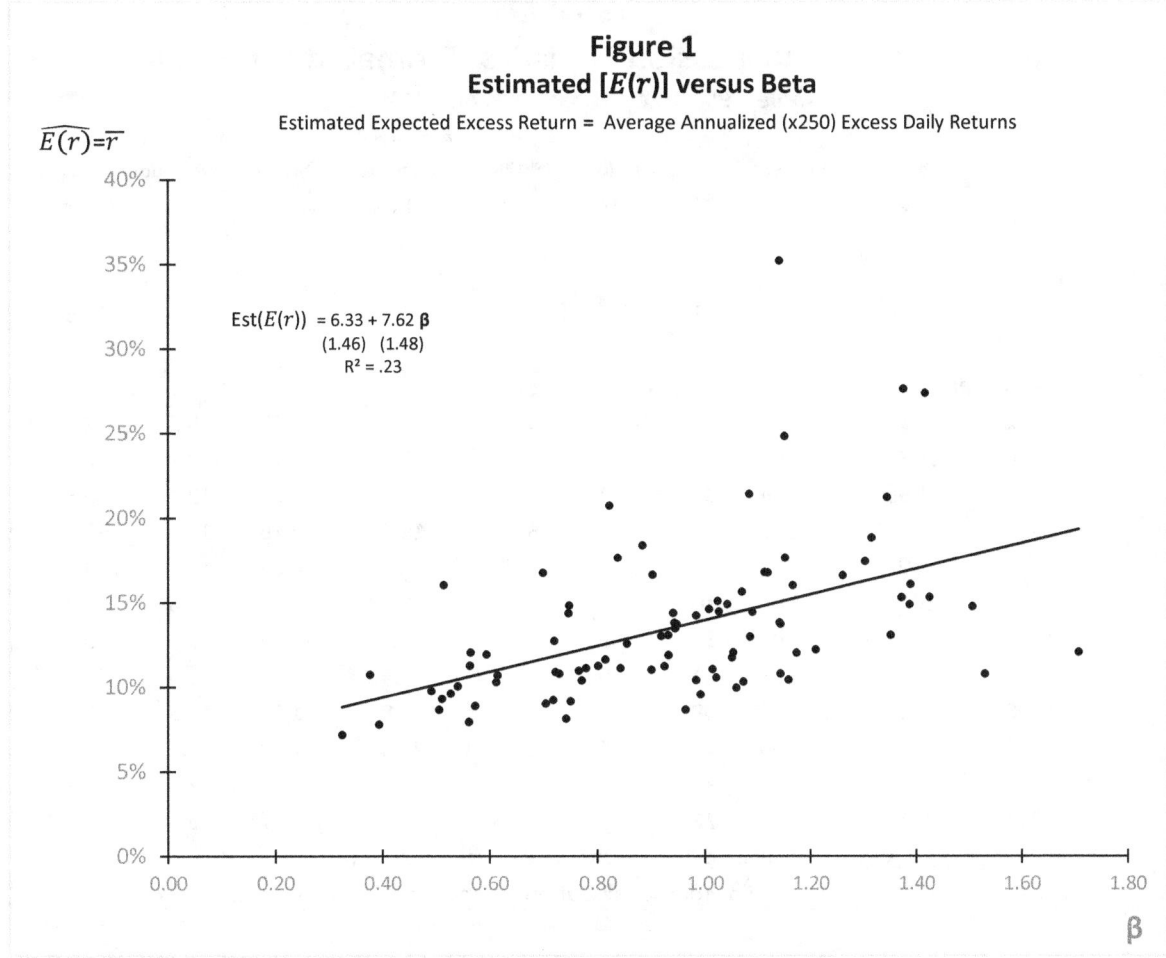

Here the intercept of 6.33%, as in other studies, is significantly different from zero (t-value under the null hypothesis that it *is* zero is 4.33)[14]. However, the slope of the security market line is not as flat as others have found. Over the period covered, the slope of 7.62% is very close to the average annualized excess return on the CRSP Index of 7.95% (t-value of -.22 in a test of the null hypothesis that they're the same – can't reject). While interesting, this really isn't the right test for the simple reason that we don't really know what the expected risk premium is for stocks. We can guess that a twenty-five year period is long enough but once again it's a function of the particular sample selected. Even if we did know the expected risk premium for stocks, over shorter periods

---

[14] Remember that we are in the world of *excess* returns (actual return minus the risk free rate), which means that a test that the intercept in non-excess return space is different from the risk-free rate (the Fama-French observation) is the same as testing that the intercept is different from *zero* here.

the slopes (see Table I) are all over the lot – ranging from -21 to 48 percentage points. The situation for two-year sub-periods is also rather cloudy for intercepts which should be close to zero (in excess return space). Only about half the time can we reject the hypothesis (and accept the alternative) that the intercept is different from zero.[15]

Table I
Cross-Sectional Regression Statistics (Estimated $E(r)$* vs. β)
Sample = 90 Largest U.S. Stocks on 12/31/2010

From (End of May)	To (End of May)	Number of Days**	R^2	Slope (β) (%)	t-value H_0: β=0	Annualized Intercept (α) (%)	t-value H_0: α=0	Average Annualized Arithmetic Returns (%) CRSP	Sample
Full Period									
1992	2016	6,046	.23	7.6	5.16	6.3	4.34	8.0	13.5
2-Year Subperiods									
1992	1994	506	.23	20.7	5.08	-9.9	-2.08	5.8	12.5
1994	1996	506	.08	11.7	2.84	8.1	1.79	17.2	20.3
1996	1998	504	.33	33.4	6.64	-10.8	-2.00	19.1	23.6
1998	2000	506	.35	47.8	6.96	-19.0	-3.16	11.0	18.7
2000	2002	500	.34	-21.3	-6.75	18.1	6.27	-13.6	3.2
2002	2004	503	.10	13.0	3.18	-1.2	-.28	6.6	11.4
2004	2006	504	.30	37.9	6.09	-23.5	-3.74	6.9	13.5
2006	2008	503	.02	7.0	1.28	4.4	.80	3.8	11.1
2008	2010	503	.08	9.7	2.84	-4.8	-1.25	-3.3	5.3
2010	2012	506	.10	-9.5	-3.12	22.5	7.08	12.7	13.2
2012	2014	501	.34	23.9	6.76	.6	.17	22.5	23.1
2014	2016	504	.22	-19.3	-5.05	25.7	6.47	6.6	6.4

*Estimated $E(r)$ = Average Annualized (x250) Arithmetic Excess Returns (AERs)
**Equal to the number of observation for the calculation of time-series betas and average excess returns.

Furthermore, there does not seem to be a ringing endorsement in Table I of the hypothesized relation between the square of the average *market* (or in this case, *index*) excess return and the size of the cross-sectional R-squared between beta and average excess return as given in equation (5). The coefficient of determination between the column labeled "R^2" in Table I and the column for CRSP (which needs to be squared in accordance with equation (5)) is a weak .23. Between R^2 and the square of the *sample* average excess returns it is weaker still (.08). Although as expected the relationship is positive (both correlation coefficients are positive). The low values are due to the fact that sample realizations of $cov(\alpha, \beta)$ definitely are not zero. For the twelve sub-periods the correlation coefficient[16] (a more accessible number which is equal to $cov(\alpha, \beta)/(\sigma_\alpha \sigma_\beta)$) ranged

---

[15] At the 99% level in a two tail test, 7 out of 12 times we can reject the null hypothesis. At the 95% level, we reject 4 out of 12 times.
[16] Not shown in Table I.

from -.61 to +.49. But even though sample realizations of $cov(\alpha, \beta)$ are not zero which obviates a clear demonstration that the success or failure of the CAPM tests is a function of the size of market index returns alone, the fact remains, obvious in Table I, that intercepts, slopes, and goodness of fit are all very much a function of a particular sample. This should not be. And it isn't, for R^2s and intercepts at least, in the tests that follow where the market's excess returns is strengthened so that the influence of beta on average excess returns shines through as predicted by equations (5).

VII. Beta vs. PAN AERs (as Estimates of Excess Expected Returns)

The comparable graph to Figure 1 is given in Figure 2 where expected excess returns estimated using **PAN AERs** are shown relative to betas:

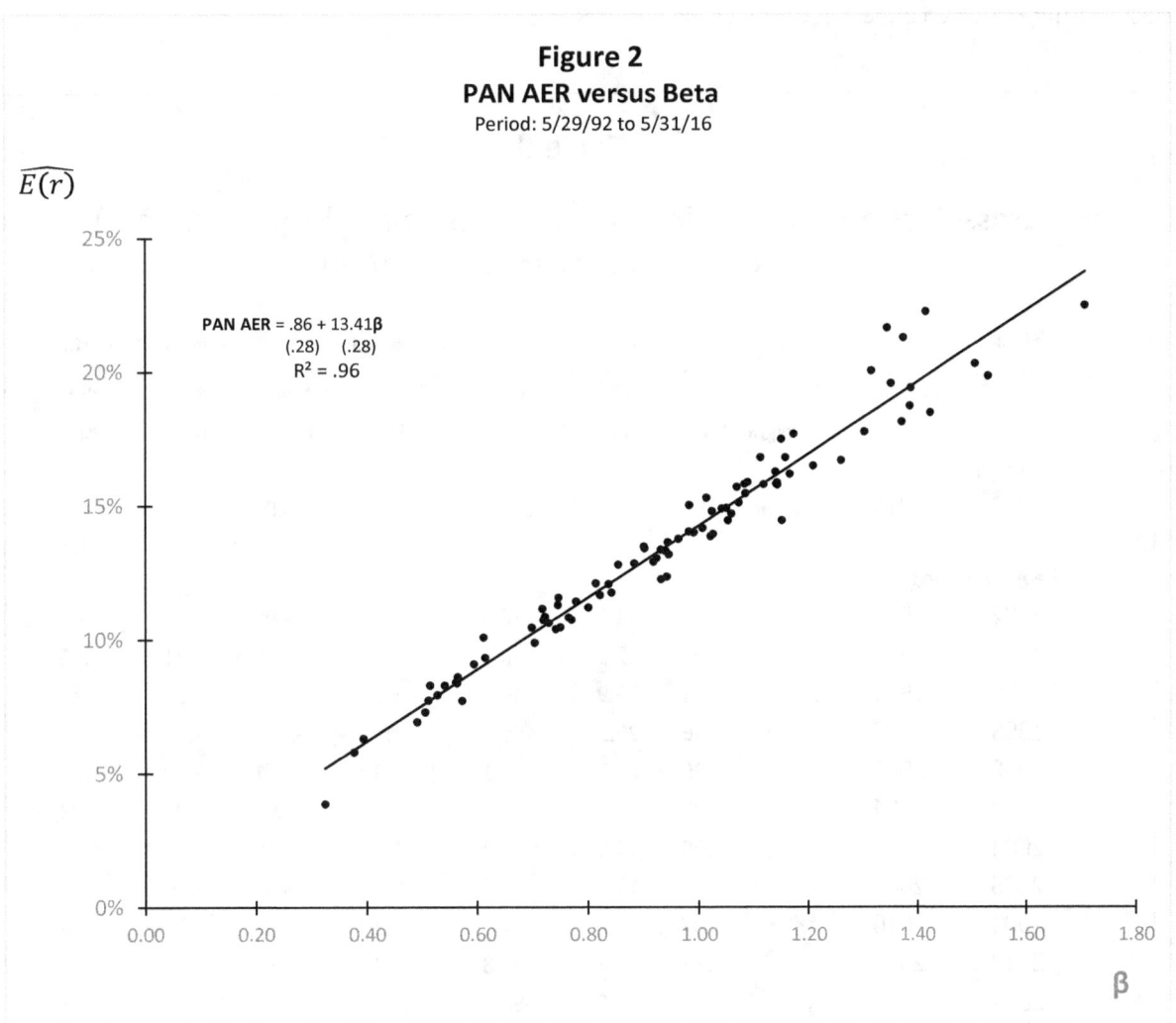

Beta is now explaining 96% of the variation in estimated expected excess returns. Before, when they were estimated using actual average excess returns (**AERs** in Figure 1) the degree of explanation was only 23%.

The intercept is now .86% which means that the estimate in this regression of a risk-free rate with a beta of zero misses the T. Bill rate by only about one percentage point. Not much of a miss when compared to the error of over 6 percentage points with AERs. In both regressions, however, the standard errors of the intercepts are such that both intercepts are statistically different from zero.

A visual inspection of Figures 1 and 2 indicates the existence of heteroscedastic disturbances: the residuals get larger as we move up the line of best fit. This condition is remedied by trimming the data to get more robust estimators; by calculating beta, for example, after having avoided a certain percent of both the biggest positive and negative daily CRSP returns and associated returns for individual stocks (see Section VIII, "A Touch of Data Mining" on page 19).

Without trimming, the results for the twelve 2-year sub-periods using **PAN AERs** is shown in Table II. As one would expect, given the dramatic improvement in the intercept and R^2 for the overall period, the drama continues in shorter periods when comparing the two methods of estimating expected excess return (**AERs** and **PAN AERs**):

Table II

Cross-Sectional Regression Statistics (Estimated $E(r)$* vs. Beta)

Sample = 90 Largest U.S. Stocks on 12/31/2010

From (End of May)	To (End of May)	Percent Pos Days (weight)	R^2	Slope (β) (%)	t-value $H_0: β=0$	Annualized Intercept (α) (%)	t-value $H_0: α=0$	Mean Daily Return for Negative Days(%)	Mean Daily Return for Positive Days(%)
Full Period									
1992	2016	54	.96	13.4	116.1	.9	3.07	-.73	.74
2-Year Subperiods									
1992	1994	53	.93	11.9	38.4	-.4	-.95	-.43	.47
1994	1996	57	.92	22.1	40.6	-2.7	-3.61	-.41	.46
1996	1998	54	.91	23.9	46.1	-1.0	-1.12	-.64	.72
1998	2000	52	.96	25.1	59.5	-1.1	-2.18	-.77	.83
2000	2002	48	.99	4.2	92.1	.3	5.71	-.70	.79
2002	2004	52	.97	11.8	56.0	.0	.02	-.92	.92
2004	2006	55	.95	14.9	46.2	-1.0	-2.75	-.51	.51
2006	2008	54	.92	10.6	43.6	1.0	3.08	-.70	.67
2008	2010	53	.97	5.4	87.7	-.3	-3.02	-1.59	1.43
2010	2012	53	.99	13.8	84.8	-.2	-1.30	-.88	.86
2012	2014	57	.95	23.6	50.4	.9	1.56	-.53	.57
2014	2016	52	.96	7.1	44.7	-.7	-4.25	-.68	.67

*Estimated $E(r)$ = Weighted Average of Normalized <u>P</u>ositive <u>A</u>nd <u>N</u>egative Average <u>E</u>xcess <u>R</u>eturns Relative to CRSP Index Positive and Negative Average Excess Returns (**PAN AERs**)

Here, intercepts ranged from -2.8% to 1.0%. Using **AERs** as shown in Table I, they ranged from -23.5% to 22.5% -- a big difference. But because the goodness-of-fit for each of the sub-periods is not very good in Table I (each regression displayed rather high intercept standard errors which were not shown), we were only able to reject the null hypothesis that the intercept was zero half the time. This is the same rejection rate for the sub-periods in Table II, which is somewhat ironic since the range of Table I sub periods intercepts is over 12 times greater than what it is for those in Table II.

Also of interest in Table II is the fact that the absolute value of the mean negative daily excess returns are very close to the mean positive daily excess returns. There's a certain very pleasing symmetry to this. It seems that the absolute size of the estimated expected excess returns that were motivating trading were virtually the same whether the market was going up or down.

Moreover, it is rather gratifying to see a high R^2 in all the twelve two-year periods as well as in the overall 24 year period. Apparently there *is* a way to test the CAPM that is not a function of a particular sample. No matter what the 2-year period, the R^2 between **PAN AERs** and betas was always above .91, (ranging from .91 to .99). And this in spite of the market being negative, -13.6% (from 5/00 to 5/02) and almost flat (5/06 to 5/08 and 5/08 to 5/10). When expected excess returns were estimated the conventional way (shown in Table I), R^2 never got above .35 and for 5 of the 12 sub periods it was at or below .10.

But it's also distressing because the consistency of the sub-period results seems to support the suspicion that what I have advanced as a way to estimate expected excess returns and therefore test the CAPM is close to a tautology. This is investigated further in Appendix B on page 33.

VII. A Monte Carlo Experiment

As already noted, realized average returns have enjoyed a prominent position as *the* way to estimate expected returns. So much so in fact that most researchers simply refer to realized returns as expected returns. But clearly they are not. They're estimates. And as estimates, they compete with the method of forming estimates advanced in this paper, what I've called the "**PAN AERs**." The obvious question is which is best? So far it would appear that **PAN AERs** are better because they are more highly correlated with betas. This might be deemed sufficient evidence. But I think it is important to demonstrate that **PAN AERs** are closer to 'true' expected excess returns (which is after all what we're after when we make estimates) than **AERs**, even with very large samples.

Of course we don't know the true expected returns. But we can create a situation where we pretend that we do and then generate pseudo **AERs** and **PAN AERs** in a large sample and see which comes closer to the "truth" and which is more correlated with beta in a Monte Carlo experiment.

Toward that end consider the following Monte Carlo setup:

1. Betas are fixed and assumed to be the true betas, β_i^{true}. They could be set to anything (between, say, .5 and 2) but to lend an air of realism I've used the actual ordinary least squares values calculated over the entire 6,046 days in the sample and forced their average to 1.00. The result is a beta range of .34 to 1.80

2. These betas are then multiplied by the average CRSP index excess return over the entire period (an annualized rate of 7.95%) which now is view as an expectation and also assumed to be true, $E(r_{index}^{true})$, to form the 90 "true" expected excess returns, $E(r_i^{true})$. Thus,

$$E(r_i^{true}) = \beta_i^{true} E(r_{index}^{true}).$$

3. All *actual* ordinary least squares residuals, $\hat{\epsilon}_{i,t}$,
$$\hat{\epsilon}_{i,t} = r_{i,t} - Intercept_i - Slope_i\, r_{index,t}$$
are calculated and stored in a 90X6046 matrix.

4. A day (*t*) from the 6,049 days in the sample is randomly selected.

5. The CRSP index excess return, $r_{index,t}$, on day *t* is then multiplied times the fixed betas, β_i^{true}, to generate the systematic portion of excess returns for all stocks.

6. Then the residual on day *t* from the 90x6046 matrix is combined with the systematic excess return from step 5 to form a "realized" excess return for all 90 stocks. This process preserves covariances among residual, as well as among excess returns across stocks but obviously destroys any auto-correlation over time that was present in the original sample.

7. Steps 4 through 6 are repeated 50,000 times (this represents 250 observations per year for 200 years).

8. Every simulated day (beyond 30) developing betas, **AERs** and **PAN AERs** are calculated.

9. Then every 250 days four values are calculated and stored:
   The R^2 between:
   1. the developing betas and the developing **AERs**
   2. the developing betas and the developing **PAN AERs**[17]

   The mean absolute deviation (MAD) between:
   3. true expected excess returns and the developing **AERs**
   4. true expected excess returns and the developing **PAN AERs**

10. Finally steps 4 through 9 are repeated 100 times so that we end up with 100 one-"year" (i.e. 250 observation) samples, 100 two-"year" (500 observation) samples, all the way out to one hundred 200-"year" samples (50,000 observation). Each year's sample is added onto the samples from previous years and the results averaged. At any "year" along the 200 "year" journey there are only 100 independent cross sectional observations of R^2s and MADs.

Notice alphas are not present, nor should they be. The idea here is to set up a situation where the CAPM is true (stable variance matrix, stable but noisy systematic excess returns and residuals) and see how long it takes to get a decent linear relationship between estimated betas and expected excess returns, estimated with either **AERs** or **PAN AERs** and also to see how long it takes for the two ways of estimating expected excess returns to converge to the truth.

A graph of the developing R^2s is shown in Figure 5. Notice the vast difference between **PAN AERs** and plain old **AERs**. For **PAN AERs** the median R^2 (heavy black line at top of the graph) is above .90 after 3 years (after 750 observations) and the range from the 5th to the 95th percentile

---

[17] Since with **PAN AERs** we don't have a direct estimate of each stock's expected return, we only have an estimate of market relative expected return, the average CRSP Index return from the random sample is multiplied times each stocks market relative expected return to get a direct estimate of expected excess return. When the process starts, the average CRSP Index return is only a poor estimate of the "true" value of 7.95%. But as the sample gets larger, the estimate gets better and better which means that if the market relative expected return is converging as well, the estimated value of each stock's expected excess returns will get close to the "true" expected excess return.

(thin black lines) is .89 to .95 after 5 years (1,250 observations). The median gets up to .96 and the range narrows to .94 to .97 after 18 years.

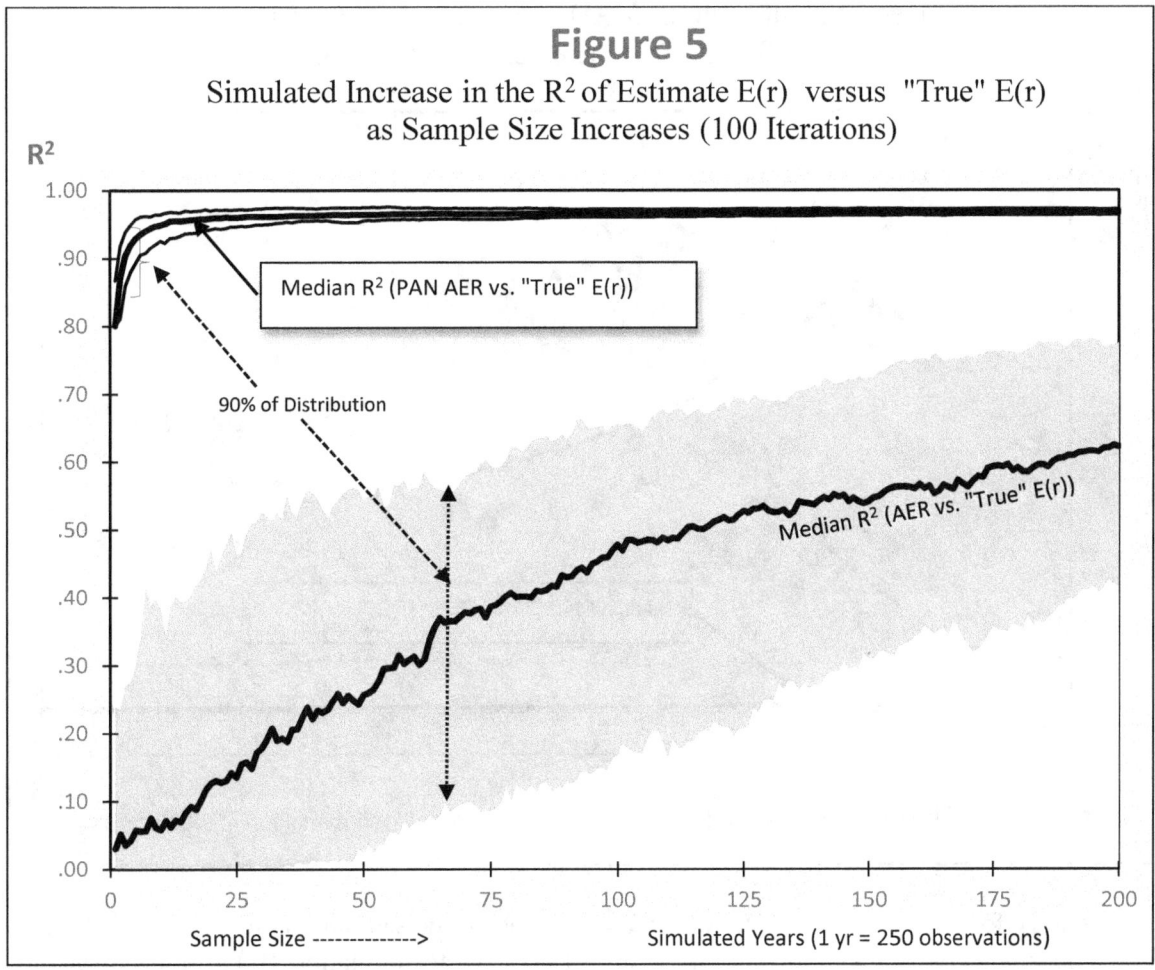

For **AERs** the story is quite different and frankly rather sad. We basically never get anywhere close to a decent R^2 – even after 200 simulated years! After 24 years (the size of the actual sample used here), the median R^2 is only up to .18 a bit less than the actual sample's .23. After 200 years is only up to .60. It's not just that samples over *fairly* long periods of time can yield **AERs** that are near zero (Elton's (1999) observation) it's that samples over *extremely* long periods do the same and thus fail to deliver results that might begin to provide evidence that the CAPM is true.

The conclusion is inescapable: R^2 between estimated expected excess returns and beta improves more rapidly with **PAN AERs** than with plain **AERs** as sample size increases.

The same pattern is evident when looking at how well the two ways for estimating expected excess returns converge to the "true" expected excess returns – a test that has nothing to do with testing the CAPM per se. Shown in Figure 6 is a graph of the developing mean absolute deviation between estimated expected excess returns and the "truth." For **PAN AERs** the average absolute deviation is down to about 50 basis points after 5 years with 90 of the 100 samples in the range of about 40 to 60 basis points. The MAD declines into the 30 to 40 basis point range by about the 35th year where it essentially remains constant.

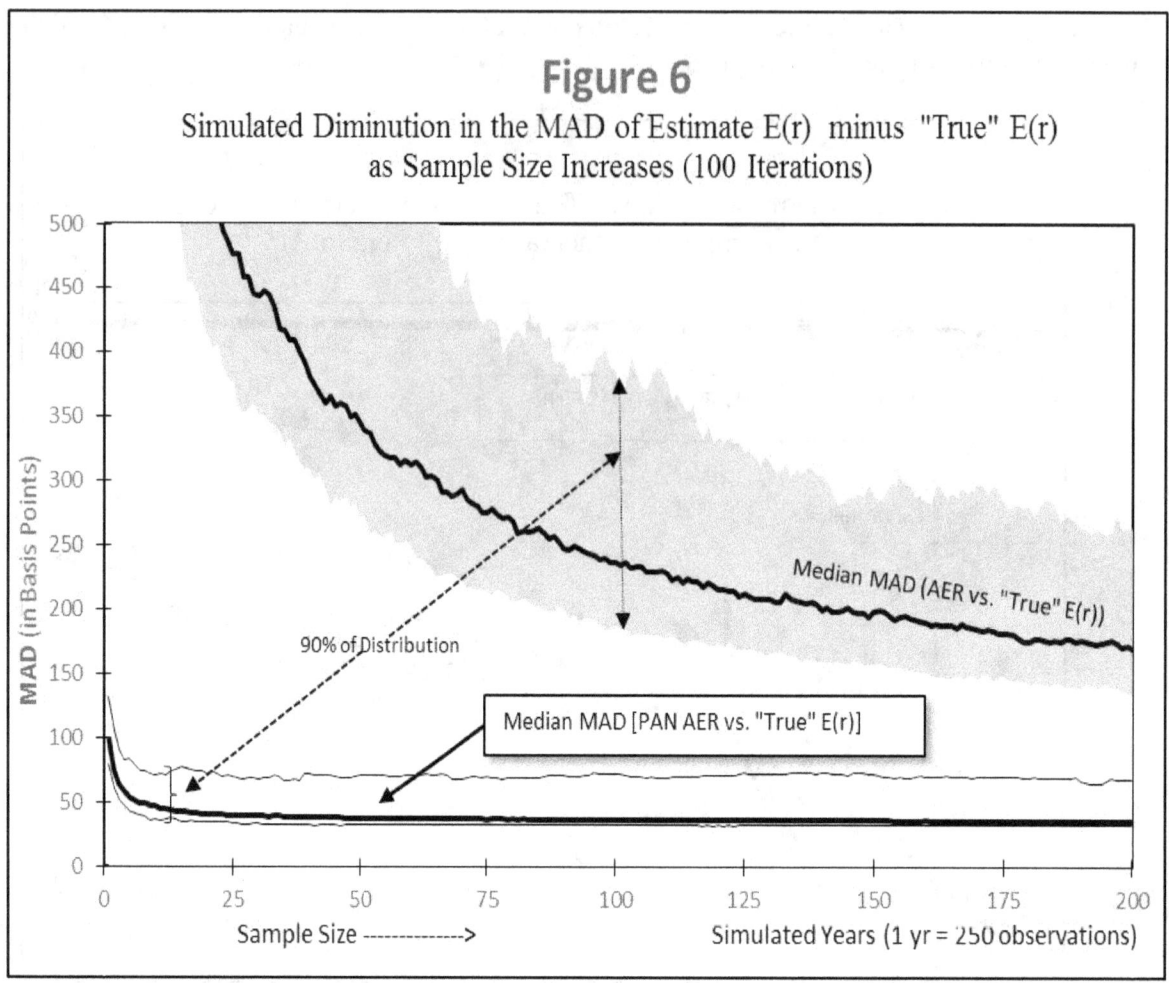

But the story for the predictive power of **AERs** continues to be sad, although it does get better as simulated time goes on. The median MAD is 174 bp after accumulating 100 samples of 50,000 observations each.

It's curious that for **PAN AERs**, R^2s and MADs don't converge to one and zero respectively. The *best* that was achieved after 200 simulated years was an R^2 of .97 (same as the median) and a MAD of 30 bp (median= 36 bp). Sampling from the actual residuals, while realistic, means that we're stuck with whatever their empirical distribution is. There's evidence that returns (and clearly the same is true for residuals) have fat tails. This is the famous Stable Paretian Hypothesis. According to Fama (1963) the hypothesis was so named by Benoit Mandelbrot who maintained that empirical distributions of price changes are closer to a family of distributions (the Cauchy distribution is one of them) that contain more of the total probability in the tails than the normal distribution. Also, their population variances are not finite which means that sample variances can be all over the lot. Could this be what's causing non-convergence? In order to find out, the Monte Carlo experiment was redone this time with sampling for the residuals from a theoretical normal distributions with mean zero and using the actual residual standard deviations, even though suspect, for each stock. Unfortunately, this procedure also breaks the back of the pattern of residual covariances (what the BARRA organization used to called and perhaps still does "extra market covariance") present in the empirical data. Thus in going from the empirical distribution of residuals to residuals that are normally distributed we've altered two major characteristics. So even if we do get convergence, and we do, we don't know which characteristic was preventing convergence before. In the end, it was deemed not worth the programming effort to try and separate out the two effects. For the record, with normally distributed residuals we did get a median MAD of 8 bp (virtually there) with a low of 5 bp and a median R^2 which went to 1.00 after the 39th year and stayed there.

It seems fair to conclude that the results of the Monte Carlo Experiment confirm the major conclusion of the empirical study that **PAN AERs** are more reliable estimates of expected excess returns than **AER** because: 1) they are more highly correlated with beta and 2) they end up getting closer to "true" expected excess returns.

VIII. A Touch of Data Mining

The heteroscedasticity that was apparent in Figure 2 seems to be related to the inclusion of excess returns out in the tails of the CRSP index distribution. In calculating beta, if the most positive 60 days and most negative 60 days for the CRSP index's excess return are trimmed (a total of 2% of the entire distribution of 6,049 daily observations, 1% avoided in each tail) and those same days are avoided for each of the 90 stocks, then the heteroscedasticity disappears as can be seen in Figure 3:

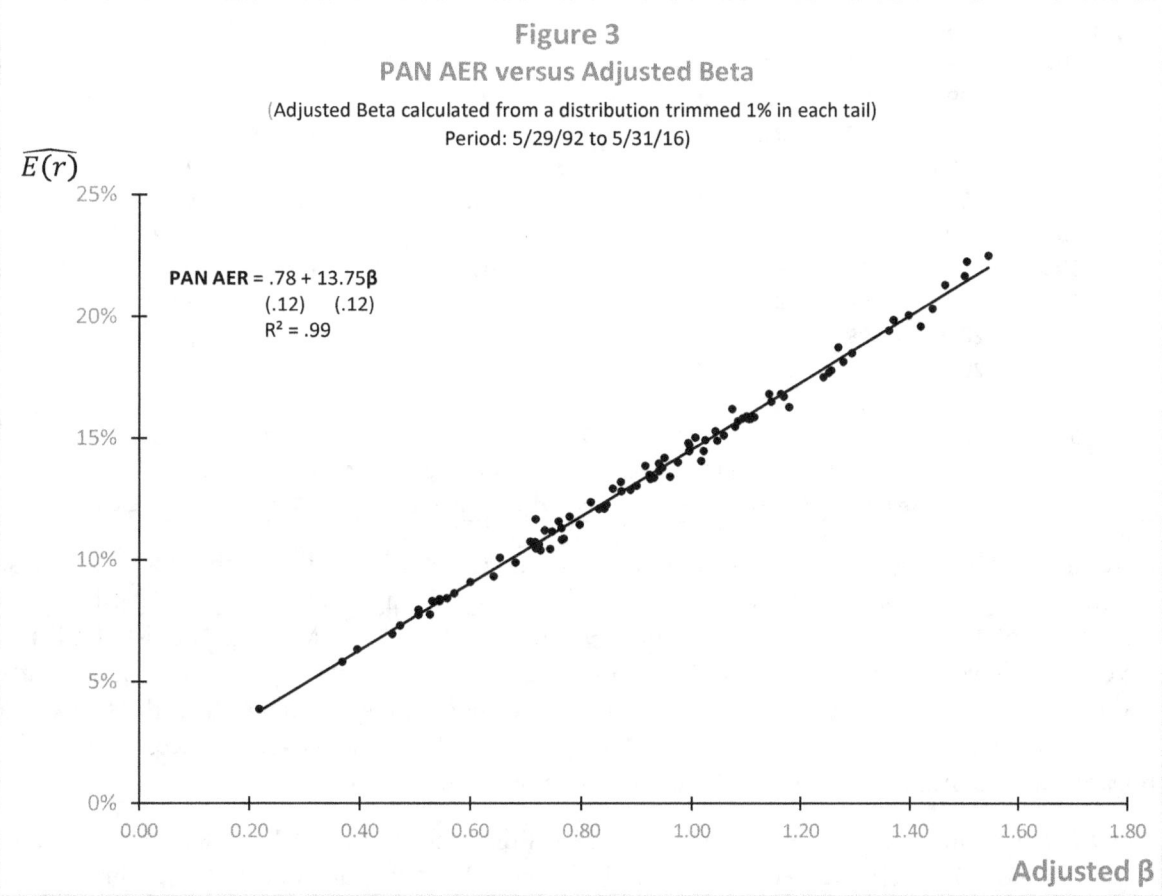

This trimming process results in a dramatic improvement. R^2 is now .99 between the "new" adjusted betas and **PAN AERs.** The whole sample of 6,049 observations was mined (shamefully!) and a 1% truncation rate for the top and bottom was found just about to be best (there's the data mining!). However, using the same truncation rate, the same direction of improvement is apparent as well in the twelve 2-years sub-periods which is shown as *Model 3* in Table III, where the results from using just **AERs** and *unadjusted* βs (*Model 1*) and using **PAN AERs** and *unadjusted* βs (*Model 2*) are repeated to facilitate comparisons. In every case R^2 either improved or stayed the same, indicating that it is a good idea to avoid extremes. But obviously a less arbitrary way of dealing with heteroscedasticity is needed.

Table III
Cross-Sectional Regression Statistics (Estimated $E(r)$* vs. β) for 3 Models
Sample = 90 Largest U.S. Stocks on 12/31/2010

Model 1: $\bar{r}_{AER}$ vs. β_{Unadj}
Model 2: $\bar{r}_{PAN\ AER}$ vs. β_{Unadj}
Model 3: $\bar{r}_{PAN\ AER}$ vs. $\beta_{Adj(1\%)}$

From (End of May)	To (End of May)	R^2 Model 1	R^2 Model 2	R^2 Model 3	Annualized Intercept (α) (%) Model 1	Model 2	Model 3	t-value (H0: α=0) Model 1	Model 2	Model 3
Full Period										
1992	2016	.23	.96	.99	6.3	.9	.8	4.34	3.07	6.77
2-Year Subperiods										
1992	1994	.23	.93	.94	-9.9	-.4	-.2	-2.08	-.95	-.43
1994	1996	.08	.92	.95	8.1	-2.7	-1.7	1.79	-3.61	-2.96
1996	1998	.33	.91	.96	-10.8	-1.0	-.5	-2.00	-1.12	-.98
1998	2000	.35	.96	.98	-19.0	-1.1	.1	-3.16	-2.18	.40
2000	2002	.34	.99	.99	18.1	.3	.0	6.27	5.71	.61
2002	2004	.10	.97	.97	-1.2	.0	.5	-.28	.02	2.27
2004	2006	.30	.95	.96	-23.5	-1.0	-.9	-3.74	-2.75	-2.65
2006	2008	.02	.92	.96	4.4	1.0	.4	.80	3.08	1.40
2008	2010	.08	.97	.99	-4.8	-.3	.3	-1.25	-3.02	4.02
2010	2012	.10	.99	.99	22.5	-.2	.1	7.08	-1.30	.63
2012	2014	.34	.95	.97	.6	.9	1.3	.17	1.56	2.77
2014	2016	.22	.96	.96	25.7	-.7	-.1	6.47	-4.25	-.66

*Estimated $E(r)$ = Weighted Average of Normalized <u>P</u>ositive <u>A</u>nd <u>N</u>egative <u>A</u>verage <u>E</u>xcess <u>R</u>eturns Relative to CRSP Index Positive and Negative Average Excess Returns (**PAN AERs**)

Here in the twelve 2-year periods a 1% truncation rate (Model 3) results in about 5 of the most negative and about 5 of the most positive CRSP index days being thrown away along with those same days for each stock. R^2s never get below .94 compared to .91 for Model 2. For Model 1, R^2s never gets *above* .35. The spread of alphas for Model 3 is 3 percentage points, for Model 2 it's about the same at 3.7. But for Model 1 it's 49.2 percentage points – greater than the spread on CRSP annualized returns which was 36.1 percentage points! No wonder average excess return/beta linearity was so dismal in Model 1. Alphas just swamped everything.

Alphas were significantly different from zero 67% of the time for Model 1, 58% for Model 2 and 42% for Model 3. We're headed in the right direction. We'd like them never to be significantly different from zero.

Throwing away observations for the beta calculation is tantamount to adjusting the entire variance matrix which has implications for where the minimum variance frontier is located and obviously where the tangency portfolio lies. It also has implications regarding the impact of other variables in explaining the residual after most of the variability in **PAN AERs** has been explained.

There apparently is a need to be very careful in estimating beta. As already noted, throwing away the most extreme observation based on what the overall market is doing as was done here is naïve and probably results in misestimating beta slightly for most stocks. But it does seem to catch the howlers and leave us with strong evidence that there is just one important factor explaining estimated excess return as the CAPM predicts. Other factors of return (the so-called "anomalies") that have gained prominence in recent years (actually, recent decades) when expected excess returns were misestimated (in my view) by average realized excess return now are much less important. How much less is a topic to which I now turn.

IX. The Anomalies

While certainly not the only anomalies that have been discovered, the 4 non-market beta factors in the Fama/French five-factor model are well known and easily accessible in the Kenneth French online Data library. They also are well documented as explaining expected excess returns (Fama and French (2014)) especially when estimated using *realized* average excess returns.

We have seen versions of two of the factors in the Fama/French (1993) 3-factor model before: SMB ("Small minus Big" a factor related to firm size) and HML ("High minus Low" a factor which places a firm on a value/growth scale, where book-to-price plays a principle role). New to the model are RMW ("Robust minus Weak" profitability) and CMA ("Conservative minus Aggressive" a factor related to low versus high investment firms).

Undoubtedly the explanatory power of these anomalies or factors of return is a function of the abject failure of beta alone to explain *realized* average excess returns. But since beta does a sterling job of explaining *expected* average excess returns as estimated by **PAN AERs**, it raises the question, is there much of a role for the anomalies? Can they explain what beta fails to explain?

An answer is provided by looking at the results from extensions of the three models already discussed, the inputs to which are generated in three passes as follows:

> **Pass 1**: Individual betas are estimated in a two-variable *time-series* (6,049 observations) regression of excess returns on the CRISP Index. In the same pass, exposures to the 4 FF factors are estimated as the coefficients in a *time-series* multiple regression of excess returns on SMB, HML, RMW, and CMA.
>
> **Pass 2**: Each stock's expected excess return as estimated by both **AERs** and **PAN AERs** are *cross-sectionally* (90 observations) regressed on its beta (calculate in the first instance using all the data and in the second with a truncated return distribution at the 1% level in each tail).
>
> **Pass 3**: Each stock's <u>residual</u> from Pass 2 is then *cross-sectionally* (again, 90 observations) regressed against each stock's exposure to the 4 FF factors (i.e., against each stock's coefficients from the time-series regressions in Pass 1).

Primarily the motivation for estimating the beta coefficient in a two variable regression and the 4 FF coefficients in a separate 5 variable multiple regression rather than all coefficients in a 6 variable multiple regression was to clearly delineate the explanatory power of beta alone and then see if the other variables explained what was left over. When there's multicollinearity in the data a multiple regression has difficulty disentangling the separate effects of independent variables. And quite frankly, since the thrust of this paper is to show that beta matters, I didn't want other variables stealing its thunder.

As can be seen in the Table IV equations describing the three models, they differ only in how the residuals are estimated in the second pass:

Table IV

(24 Years of Daily Data from 5/29/92 to 5/31/16)

Pass 1: Individual βs estimated in a 2 variable regression of excess returns on CRSP Index. Coefficients (SMB, HML, RMW, CMA) estimated in a multiple regression of excess returns on the 4 (non-beta) Fama/French factor returns.

Pass 2: Estimated expected returns (AERs and PAN AERs) regressed on βs from Pass 1.

Pass 3: Residual from Pass 2 regressed on the 4 (non-beta) Fama/French factor coefficients.

Model 1:

Pass 2 (R^2= .23): $\bar{r}_{i,AER} = \hat{\gamma}_0 + \hat{\gamma}_1 \beta_i^{unadj} + \hat{\varepsilon}_{i,AER}$

Pass 3 (R^2= .46): $\hat{\varepsilon}_{i,AER} = \hat{\gamma}_0 + \hat{\gamma}_1 SMB_i + \hat{\gamma}_2 HML_i + \hat{\gamma}_3 RMW_i + \hat{\gamma}_4 CMA_i + \hat{e}_i$

Model 2:

Pass 2 (R^2= .96): $\bar{r}_{i,PAN\ AER} = \hat{\gamma}_0 + \hat{\gamma}_1 \beta_i^{unadj} + \hat{\varepsilon}_{i,PAN\ AER}$

Pass 3 (R^2= .67): $\hat{\varepsilon}_{i,PAN\ AER} = \hat{\gamma}_0 + \hat{\gamma}_1 SMB_i + \hat{\gamma}_2 HML_i + \hat{\gamma}_3 RMW_i + \hat{\gamma}_4 CMA_i + \hat{e}_i$

Model 3:

Pass 2 (R^2= .99): $\bar{r}_{i,PAN\ AER} = \hat{\gamma}_0 + \hat{\gamma}_1 \beta_i^{adj} + \hat{\varepsilon}_{i,PAN\ AER}$

Pass 3 (R^2= .15): $\hat{\varepsilon}_{i,PAN\ AER} = \hat{\gamma}_0 + \hat{\gamma}_1 SMB_i + \hat{\gamma}_2 HML_i + \hat{\gamma}_3 RMW_i + \hat{\gamma}_4 CMA_i + \hat{e}_i$

	Pass 2			Pass 3				
	$\hat{\gamma}_0$	$\hat{\gamma}_1$		$\hat{\gamma}_0$	$\hat{\gamma}_1$	$\hat{\gamma}_2$	$\hat{\gamma}_3$	$\hat{\gamma}_4$
Coefficients								
Model 1	6.33	7.62		1.86	5.69	-4.88	.43	-3.45
Model 2	.86	13.41		.35	.23	-1.23	.11	-.74
Model 3	.78	13.75		-.02	-.04	.00	.28	-.29
t-Values			R^2					R^2
Model 1	4.34	5.16	.23	4.49	3.93	-7.49	.44	-3.64	.46
Model 2	3.07	47.52	.96	5.60	1.07	-12.53	.77	-5.21	.67
Model 3	6.77	116.08	.99	-.42	-.27	-.07	2.86	-3.10	.15

The benchmark case is Model 1, where in pass 2 average excess returns, $\bar{r}_{i,AER}$, are regressed on unadjusted betas, β_i^{unadj}, and then what beta failed to explain, the estimated *residuals*, $\hat{\varepsilon}_{i,AER}$, are regressed on the 4 FF factors in the third pass. As has already been pointed out, unadjusted beta in the second pass explains a tepid 23% of the variation in average excess returns. The 4 FF factors in the third pass then pick up the slack and explain almost half (46%) of what β didn't explain in the second pass. Based on the t-values under the null hypothesis that the coefficients are zero, in all but one (RMW) of the 4 FF factor coefficients the null hypothesis is rejected – the coefficients are statistically significant. Since the approach here is very different from the approach taken by Fama and French (2015) their results are not directly comparable to the results for model 1.[18]

It starts to get interesting in Model 2 when **PAN AERs** are used in place of just average excess returns. In the second pass, beta, which is highly significant with a t-value of 47.52, explains 96% of the variation in **PAN AERs**. Of the remaining 4% of the total variation left unexplained, the 4 FF factors do a good job ($R^2 = .67$), but look what happens to the size of the coefficients themselves. They get very small indeed. And another factor (SMB) lapses into statistical insignificance.

This pattern continues when the "data mined" adjusted betas are used along with **PAN AERs**. Now there is only 1% of the total variation left unexplained after pass 2. In pass 3, another one (HML) of the original factors in the Fama/French 3 variables factor model joins the size variable (SMB) in statistical insignificance. RMW, the profitability factor, is now significant but not wildly so. The other "new" factor relating to investments (CMA) continues to negatively influence expected excess returns as estimated with **PAN AERs** on the 90 large cap stocks used here. Robust profitably and aggressive investments give a consistent boost to expected excess returns when betas are estimated with trimmed data.

Even without resorting to the data mined results in Model 3 and in spite of the 4 FF factors explaining 2/3 of what was left unexplained from pass 2 in Model 2, it's tempting to discount the role of these 4 anomalies in explaining estimated expected excess returns. They did after all have to explain only 4% of the total variation of **PAN AERs** in Model 2.

Another issue with the 4 Fama/French factors is their stability. If indeed these factors represent undiversifiable risks, then when we look at many shorter periods, there should be a fairly consistent positive reward (negative for CMA) for bearing these risks. But this is not the case as can be seen in the first part of Table V where the results from 12 two-year sub periods for Models 1 and 3 are presented side by side. In Model 1 the coefficients in the 3rd pass on SMB, HML, RMW, and CMA are negative 33%, 50% 58% and 42% of the time respectively. In Model 3 the percentages are; 33%, 33%, 58% and 33%.

The sign on the coefficient for β goes from positive (which it should be) to negative 25% of the time in Model 1. In contrast, the coefficient on adjusted beta in the 2nd pass of Model 3 is *always positive*, indicating that investors consistently expect to be rewarded for bearing market risk even though that reward varies considerably. It ranges from 4.4% to 24.2%, but is always statistically significant. The t-value on the coefficient for β as seen in the second part of Table V never gets below 38.4.

---

[18]In short, different data, different time periods and different approach. In this study daily data from 5/29/92 to 5/31/2016 on the 90 largest stocks without aggregation into portfolios are used whereas the Fama French (2015) study uses monthly data from July, 1963 to December, 2013 for all NYSE, Amex and NASDAQ stocks on both CRSP and Compustat and aggregates these data into portfolios to maximize the spread on the variables of interest and ameliorate errors-in-variables problems

Table V

Coefficients (and R^2s)

	Model 1: $\bar{r}_{AER}$ vs. β_{Unadj}								Model 3: $\bar{r}_{PAN\,AER}$ vs. $\beta_{Adj(1\%)}$							
	Intercept	Slope	R^2	Intercept	SMB	HML	RMW	CMA	R^2	Intercept	Slope	R^2	Intercept	SMB	HML	RMW	CMA	R^2
5/92 - 5/16	6.3	7.6	.23	1.2	5.9	-4.9	.7	-3.1	.45	.8	13.8	.99	.0	.0	.0	.3	-.3	.15
2-year periods ending at the end of May																		
1994	-9.9	20.7	.23	6.2	12.6	5.0	-8.0	.1	.35	-.2	11.5	.94	.3	.5	-.3	.1	.1	.10
1996	8.1	11.7	.08	2.2	3.5	-5.8	5.4	-.9	.18	-1.7	21.1	.95	-.9	-.1	-1.0	.0	-.1	.12
1998	-10.8	33.4	.33	4.8	-7.3	8.2	3.4	1.3	.21	-.5	23.5	.96	-.6	.2	-.5	-.2	-.1	.05
2000	-19.0	47.8	.35	10.9	24.2	-15.1	-30.1	6.0	.52	.1	24.2	.98	-.5	-1.0	.5	.9	-.5	.20
2002	18.1	-21.3	.34	6.6	9.9	1.1	7.4	.1	.09	.0	4.4	.99	.0	.1	.0	-.2	.0	.11
2004	-1.2	13.0	.10	13.3	27.0	2.9	-9.0	3.3	.43	.5	11.5	.97	.1	.2	.1	-.2	.1	.04
2006	-23.5	37.9	.30	-.1	-4.1	5.3	-3.8	-6.5	.40	-.9	14.9	.96	.3	-.1	.2	-.1	.4	.09
2008	4.4	7.0	.02	1.6	-8.6	-5.2	-1.2	-8.6	.31	.4	11.3	.96	-.2	.2	-.3	-.1	-.2	.12
2010	-4.8	9.7	.08	-2.3	10.3	6.2	1.7	4.3	.24	.3	4.9	.99	.1	.3	.0	.0	.0	.15
2012	22.5	-9.5	.10	-1.0	11.9	-4.9	3.3	-1.4	.16	.1	13.4	.99	.0	-.2	.4	-.1	.2	.16
2014	.6	23.9	.34	-.6	1.1	-4.0	-4.0	.4	.18	1.3	23.3	.97	-.1	.2	1.1	-.2	.8	.23
2016	25.7	-19.3	.22	-3.4	-2.5	-12.2	-4.1	-8.5	.48	-.1	6.5	.96	.1	.3	.2	.0	.2	.19

Overall the t-values on the 4 Fama/French factors for the 12 two-year periods in Model 3 get above 2.0 (significant at the 99% level) 21% percent of the time and below -2.0 8 % of the time.

Table V - continued

Coefficient t-Values (H_0: Coefficient=0)

	Model 1: $\bar{r}_{AER}$ vs. β_{Unadj}							Model 3: $\bar{r}_{PAN\,AER}$ vs. $\beta_{Adj(1\%)}$						
	Intercept	Slope	Intercept	SMB	HML	RMW	CMA	Intercept	Slope	Intercept	SMB	HML	RMW	CMA
5/92 - 5/16	4.3	5.2	2.0	4.0	-7.4	.8	-3.5	6.8	116.1	-.4	-.2	-.1	3.1	-3.1
2-year periods ending at the end of May														
1994	-2.1	5.1	2.1	4.3	2.6	-4.2	.1	-.4	38.4	1.1	1.9	-1.9	.8	1.1
1996	1.8	2.8	.5	1.0	-2.7	3.2	-.8	-3.0	40.6	-1.5	-.1	-3.4	.1	-.4
1998	-2.0	6.6	.9	-2.0	3.3	2.0	.7	-1.0	46.1	-.9	.4	-1.8	-1.0	-.5
2000	-3.2	7.0	2.7	4.7	-4.9	-6.9	1.9	.4	59.5	-1.6	-2.4	2.2	2.5	-2.1
2002	6.3	-6.7	1.6	1.4	.3	2.1	.1	.6	92.1	1.6	2.6	-1.3	-3.6	-.8
2004	-.3	3.2	4.6	7.6	1.5	-5.5	1.7	2.3	56.0	.4	1.0	1.1	-1.7	.8
2006	-3.7	6.1	.0	-1.0	2.8	-1.5	-3.2	-2.6	46.2	1.3	-.5	1.7	-.5	2.9
2008	.8	1.3	.5	-2.0	-2.1	-.5	-5.7	1.4	43.6	-1.2	.9	-2.6	-.5	-2.6
2010	-1.2	2.8	-1.1	2.6	3.6	.7	2.9	4.0	87.7	1.3	3.5	-1.3	.5	-.9
2012	7.1	-3.1	-.4	2.3	-2.2	1.5	-.5	.6	84.8	-.2	-.8	3.7	-.8	1.2
2014	.2	6.8	-.3	.3	-2.0	-2.4	.2	2.8	50.4	-.3	.4	4.2	-1.0	4.4
2016	6.5	-5.0	-2.3	-.6	-6.6	-2.6	-6.0	-.7	44.7	.9	1.3	2.1	-.5	2.7

X. The Tangency Portfolio

A sufficient condition for the CAPM to be true would be finding that all the weights in the tangency portfolio were identical to the weights in the market portfolio. But since we don't know the composition of the market portfolio and probably never will (Roll's point), we have to be content with comparing the tangency portfolio to a constant-weight index of stocks, pretending as if it is the market portfolio. We know that if markets clear, the market portfolio (and our index) cannot contain short positions, because if it did it would not be the sum of all portfolios (or, in the case of the index, would not have weights based on shares outstanding). So if the tangency portfolio is "close" to the index, it shouldn't have very many short positions, if any at all. Moreover what positions it does have, should not be very different from those in the index. The mean absolute deviation should not be large. And finally there should be a positive, and hopefully high, correlation between the two sets of weights.

Weights in the tangency portfolio are only a function of expected excess returns and the variance matrix (see equation (A6) in Appendix A). As developed above there are two sets of expected excess returns: those estimated by **AERs** and those estimated by **PAN AERs** and two versions of the variance/covariance matrix: one estimated using all the data and the other estimated with individual stock excess returns avoided on days when the CRSP index had its largest positive and negative moves (60 days each). For determining the mean absolute deviation (in basis points in Table VI) and the correlation of index weights *versus* tangency portfolio weights, the former were taken as the weights as of 12/31/2010 in an index of the 90 stocks in the study (see the capitalization column in Appendix C):

TABLE VI
Tangency Portfolio Reasonableness

Var/Cov Estimated using	Expected Excess Returns Estimated using	Tangency Portfolio Weights Min	Max	% Short	Tangency Port Wgts. Vs. Cap Wgts for 90 Stock Port MAD	Correlation
All the Data						
	AERs	-18.5%	28.0%	47	586	-.10
	PAN AERs	-4.3%	6.0%	26	153	.02
Truncated Data						
	AERs	-13.9%	21.7%	43%	480	-.08
	PAN AERs	-2.8%	4.3%	12%	97	.17

As expected, use of **PAN AERs** rather than just plain **AERs** results in a far more reasonable tangency portfolio. With all the data, estimating expected excess returns using realized average excess returns (**AERs**) results in almost half of the positions being short (47%)[19] and a huge spread of 56.5 percentage points between the minimum weight (-18.5%) and the maximum weight (28%). What minimal relationship there is (coefficient of correlation = -.1) between tangency portfolio weights and end of the year 2010 capitalization weights has the wrong sign. It should be positive. Clearly, this way of estimating expected excess returns results in a tangency portfolio that is unreasonable. But is it dramatically different with **PAN AERs** as estimates? Well, not dramatically, but we are on the right road. Again, as expected, given the improvement in beta/return linearity that we've already seen, it's not surprising that all reasonableness measures improve.

And they get better still when the truncated data is used. Not only are just 12% of the weights negative, the spread from minimum to maximum is 7.1 percentage points which compares favorably to the spread of 5.3 percentage points in the actual 2010 capitalization weights. Are we there? Recall that we don't want a perfect fit, because then the variance matrix as estimated from actual data and the **PAN AER** way of estimating expected excess returns would imply that trading would screech to a halt or at least proceed very slowly with only a desire for liquidity motivating it. No, we need something less than perfect.

Of all the measures of reasonableness, the percentage of short positions might seem the most "reasonable," if you will. We know that all positions in the elusive "market portfolio" are positive, so it would seem that the fewer short positions in a tangency portfolio we calculate the closer it must be to the market portfolio. Yet we know we will never really get there. Even if the expected returns on the subset of assets (the stocks) that we're investigating were exactly correct (i.e., linearly related to betas calculated off the true market portfolio), without expected returns on the full cohort of assets (the stamp collections, the jewels, the antique cars, etc.) it seems entirely possible we might find a tangency portfolio that has short positions. Some of those short positions might just be compensating for all the missing assets. But even if they are not. We know the whole process is extremely sensitive to slight variations in the basic parameters. This is a point that Roll and Ross make at the end of their 1994 paper:

> The almost pathological knife-edge nature of the expected return-beta OLS cross-sectional relation, even without measurement error, is a shaky base for modern finance.

To which I can add the following *ad hoc* test regarding the composition of the tangency portfolio. If expected returns are estimated as just beta, or, if you like, beta times a market expected return -- it comes to the same thing; it's just a matter of scale -- and those betas are estimated against an index of 2010 capitalization weights, rebalanced every day, then the tangency portfolio weights will be identical to the weights in the index (See appendix A). However, if those very same betas are rounded to two decimals and plugged in as expected excess returns, the tangency portfolio with the historical variance matrix has two short positions (2%), a maximum position of 4.7% vs 5.6% in the index, a MAD of 22 basis points and a correlation of .95 with the actual cap weights. More or less the same results obtain if one takes beta times a market excess return of 8.0% and rounds to one decimal (two shorts, a maximum position of 5.3%, MAD of 23 bp, and a correlation of .96).

Thus it is not surprising that we end up with short positions in the tangency portfolio.

---

[19] This is almost exactly in line with the Levy and Ritov (2011) empirical simulation results. They find that "... the percentage of stocks held short in the optimal portfolios converges to 50% as the number of assets increases." (p. 1468). For 90 stocks, as I read their graph, the percentage looks like 45%.

XI. Conclusion

Much has been made of the inability of beta to explain average experienced excess returns. The relationship is too flat (Fama/French (2004)). The relationship is suspect to begin with – could be reversed if another inefficient index were used (Roll and Ross (1984)). But in spite of all this the CAPM has endured, no doubt because it has the ring of truth to it, especially for stocks What's generally been missing in most of the tests to date is a recognition that the theory is not about explaining what's happened—what returns have been realized – but about what's expected to happen. What's happened on average is surely a guide in forming expectations. But it can't be the entire story. And it isn't. If nothing else, the formation of expectation is a bit more nuanced.

Perhaps if we had looked at how expectations are formed in extreme conditions (in the cauldron of a serious bear market, for example), we'd have concluded, even before testing, that of course the CAPM was true. Of course the market, when it makes big moves, differentially moves all stocks. Who would expect anything different? But the theory is silent on expectation formation. From the CAPM view point, it is assumed that somehow investors come to market with a well formed, rather precise, notion of each stock's expected value and that *all investors share the same expectation.* Rather heroic this.

A more likely scenario is that investors assess the way stocks behave in different market conditions. Bank stocks, for example, seem to go down in bear markets consistently more than utilities. Rational investors would be hard pressed not to *expect* similar behavior in the future. The expectation might take the form that banks are expected to go down around 15% more than the general market and utilities around 20% less. Utilities are thus seen as less risky than banks. In other words, in this scenario banks have a beta of about 1.15 and utilities, about .80 when the market (as measured by a broadly based index like the S&P 500, or the Russell 3000 or, horrors, even the Dow) is seriously down.

Now, if investors are really worried about the probability of loss then they will avoid go-down-more-than-the-market-in-bear-markets type stocks even in good times causing their prices to fall until such time that the expectation in bull markets (which are expected to inevitably come and last longer) is enough to more than compensate for the loss in bear markets. In such a scenario do investors need to have homogeneous expectations in the sense that they all have access to the same investment information and come to the same conclusion? No. All they need to have is more or less homogeneous observational skills. For example, as the market falls, a single investor will notice, but not perhaps know why, that other investors have bid down the prices of bank stocks more than utilities, reasoning that it's just something the cognoscenti do. And all investors are going to be keenly aware of the same thing and form an expectation for good times as well as bad based on it. Nothing concentrates the mind like loss.

The formation of relative expected returns in down markets and the virtual mirror image in up markets is the main point of this paper. It's a point made in reference to the problems of empirically testing the CAPM, but it's a point that could easily be applied to what investors look at in forming an expected excess return in the first place. It's not that investors all think the same. It's that they all worry about the same thing: a stock's potential behavior in a serious bear market. And if that worry, based as it must be, on *past* price behavior in bear markets, is reflected in current trading then it seems reasonable to assume that what investors expect in bull markets has to compensate not only for what they might potentially lose in bear markets but also for the sleepless nights contemplating all the bad things that might happen. If it doesn't, then the price falls until it does. Could it be that the CAPM conclusion of a single factor driving expected returns is embedded in the way expectations are formed? Was it staring us in the face all along? It certainly seems from this empirical investigation as if non-market, non-beta related influences on expected returns (including alphas) are ephemeral – interesting, but ultimately distracting arpeggios weaving in and out of the main CAPM theme: equilibrium in capital markets driven by beta alone.

Appendix A [20]

Step 1: Optimal Portfolio Construction:

$$Min: w'_{tan} V w_{tan}, \; s.t.: w'_{tan} \mu = \theta_{tan}$$

Where:
- $\mu \equiv$ Column vector of expected <u>excess</u> returns $\equiv E(R) - \iota \, r_f$
- $E(R) \equiv$ Column vector of expected returns,
- $r_f \equiv$ Risk-free rate,
- $\iota \equiv$ Column vector of conformable 1's
- $w \equiv$ Column vector of portfolio weights,
- $V \equiv$ Variance matrix, and
- $\theta_{tan} \equiv$ Expected excess return of the "tangency" portfolio $= E(R_{tan}) - r_f$

$$\mathcal{L} = w'_{tan} V w_{tan} + \delta(\theta_{tan} - w'_{tan} \mu) \qquad \text{Form the Lagrangian, } \mathcal{L}$$

$$\frac{\partial \mathcal{L}}{\partial w_{tan}} = 2 V w_{tan} + \delta(-\mu) = 0 \qquad \text{Differentiate and set to 0} \qquad (A1)$$

$$w_{tan} = (\delta V^{-1} \mu)/2 \qquad \text{Solve (A1) for } w_{tan} \qquad (A2)$$

$$\mu' w_{tan} = (\delta \mu' V^{-1} \mu)/2 \qquad \text{Premultiply (A2) by } \mu' \qquad (A3)$$

$$\delta = \frac{2\theta_{tan}}{\mu' V^{-1} \mu} \qquad \text{Solve (A3) for } \delta \text{ and note that: } w'_{tan} \mu = \theta_{tan} \qquad (A4)$$

$$w_{tan} = \left(\frac{\theta_{tan}}{\mu' V^{-1} \mu}\right) V^{-1} \mu \qquad \text{Substitute (A4) into (A2)}$$

$$W_{tan} \equiv \frac{w_{tan}}{\iota' w_{tan}} \qquad \text{Define new weights, so } \iota' W_{tan} = 1$$

$$\therefore \quad W_{tan} = \frac{V^{-1} \mu}{\iota' V^{-1} \mu} \qquad \text{Since } \iota' w_{tan} = \left(\frac{\theta_{tan}}{\mu' V^{-1} \mu}\right) \iota' V^{-1} \mu \qquad (A6)$$

---

[20] This proof was cobbled together from several sources, but primarily from Campbell, Lo & MacKinlay (1997, p.187).

Step 2: Derive the CAPM (where markets clear, etc.)

$$w_{mkt} = w_{tan} \qquad \text{Since } w_{tan} \text{ is the same for all investors} \qquad (A7)$$

$$0 = 2w'_{mkt} V w_{mkt} - \delta(w'_{mkt}\mu) \qquad \text{Substitute (A7) into (A1) \& premultiply by } w'_{mkt} \qquad (A8)$$

$$\delta = \frac{2w'_{mkt} V w_{mkt}}{w'_{mkt}\mu} \qquad \text{Solve (A8) for } \delta \qquad (A9)$$

$$0 = 2V w_{mkt} - \frac{2w'_{mkt} V w_{mkt}}{w'_{mkt}\mu}\mu \qquad \text{Substitute (A7) and (A9) into (A1)}$$

$$0 = V W_{mkt} - \frac{W'_{mkt} V W_{mkt}}{\theta_{mkt}}\mu \qquad \text{Since } W_{mkt} \equiv \frac{w_{mkt}}{\iota' w_{mkt}} \text{ and } \theta_{mkt} = w'_{mkt}\mu \qquad (A10)$$

$$\mu = \frac{V W_{mkt}}{W'_{mkt} V W_{mkt}}\theta_{mkt} \qquad \text{Solve (A10) for } \mu \qquad (A11)$$

$$E(R) = \iota r_f + \frac{V W_{mkt}}{W'_{mkt} V W_{mkt}}[E(R_{mkt}) - r_f] \;,\; \text{Since } \mu = E(R) - \iota r_f \text{ and } \theta_{mkt} = E(R_{mkt}) - r_f$$

$$\therefore \quad E(R) = \iota r_f + \beta_{mkt}[E(R_{mkt}) - r_f] \;, \qquad \text{where: } \beta_{mkt} \equiv \frac{V W_{mkt}}{W'_{mkt} V W_{mkt}}$$

Proof that expected excess return/beta linearity and market portfolio mean- variance efficiency are logically equivalent

To prove logical equivalence, it's necessary to prove a bi-conditional (*i.e.,* an 'if and only if' relation), $p \equiv q$, which is the same as $p \supset q \cdot q \supset p$ (Quine (1959), p.16). For the case we're considering here we need to prove that efficiency (p) implies linearity (q) **and** linearity (q) implies efficiency (p).

So let's start by showing that linearity follows from efficiency. That is, let's assume that weights, W_{index}, in some arbitrary portfolio, P_{index}, are equal to the weights, W_{tan}, in a mean/variance efficient tangency portfolio, P_{tan}. This means P_{index} is efficient as well which in turn means that, from equation (A6) above, we are **assuming**:

$$W_{index} = \frac{V^{-1}\mu}{\iota' V^{-1}\mu} \tag{A12}$$

where the non-singular variance matrix, V, and the expected excess return vector, μ, are both exogenously determined.

From this assumption we need to prove that the betas, β_{index} defined relative to V and to the portfolio (or index, if you will) P_{index} are linearly related to the excess return vector, μ. In another words we need to **prove**:

$$\beta_{index} = k\mu \tag{A13}$$

where k is a scalar, which is to say that it is a constant and the same for all stocks.

Premultipy (A12) by V and then divide both sides by the scalar $W'_{index} V W_{index}$:

$$\frac{V W_{index}}{W'_{index} V W_{index}} = \left[\frac{1}{\iota' V^{-1}\mu \; W'_{index} V W_{index}}\right]\mu \tag{A14}$$

The left hand side of equation (A14) is equal to the definition of β_{index} defined against the portfolio P_{index} (which is an index with constant weights) and the expression in the square brackets is a scalar which can be set equal to k, thereby **proving** the first half of the bi-conditional.

The second half proceeds in a similar manner. Start with equation (A13) as the assumption.

That is, **assume**:
$$\beta_{index} = k\mu \tag{A13'}$$

and then, **prove**:
$$W_{index} = W_{tan}.$$

Substitute the definition of beta into the assumption (A13'):

$$\frac{V W_{index}}{W'_{index} V W_{index}} = k\mu \qquad (A15)$$

Premultiply both sides of (A15) by V^{-1}:

$$\frac{V^{-1} V W_{index}}{W'_{index} V W_{index}} = V^{-1} k\mu \qquad (A16)$$

and then multiply both sides of (A16) by the scalar $W'_{index} V W_{index}$ to get:

$$W_{index} = k (W'_{index} V W_{index}) V^{-1} \mu \qquad (A17)$$

Finally, multiply the right hand side of (A17) by $\dfrac{i'V^{-1}\mu}{i'V^{-1}\mu}$ and use (A6) to get:

$$W_{index} = [k(i'V^{-1}\mu)(W'_{index} V W_{index})] W_{tan}$$

Then, since $k = \left[\dfrac{1}{(i'V^{-1}\mu)\,(W'_{index} V W_{index})}\right]$,

$$W_{index} = W_{tan}$$

QED.

Appendix B

So, How Tautological Is All This?

What makes it seem as if we are heading towards a tautology is the presence of alphas and their diminished impact as we move away from the center of the excess return distribution. If all alphas were zero, then, yes, we would have a tautology: there would be an exact positive linear relationship between **AERs** and betas which means that the index we used as the regressor in calculating betas would indeed be an efficient portfolio and in fact would be the tangency portfolio.

But in the real world a high alpha for a stock with a low beta could very easily have a higher average excess return that another stock with a negative alpha but a high beta. For these two stocks, there would be a *negative* relationship between **AERs** and betas. For **PAN AERs** such a situation could arise but it is less likely. Alphas just don't have as much impact when excess returns are measured out in the tails of the distribution. The total alpha does get partitioned, but the absolute value of the size of each partitions is small when compared to the absolute value of the size of the excess returns for positive and negative market days. When we look at returns in the tails of the distribution alphas simply aren't on the same scale. The anecdotal evidence is readily available. Consider the results for two bank stocks: Wells Fargo and Bank of America:

	Wells Fargo	Bank of America
Beta	1.26	1.53
Daily Mean Excess Return (bp)		
Overall	7	4
Negative Markets	-91	-111
Positive Markets	91	105
Alphas (bp)		
Overall	3	-1
(mkt<=0)	11	12
(mkt>0)	-4	-11

Wells Fargo has a lower beta (1.26) but a higher overall average excess return (7 bp) than Bank of America's higher beta (1.53) but lower overall average excess return (4 bp) – a negative mean/beta relationship. But when we move to the average excess return on days when the market is positive, the higher beta (1.53) of B of A goes with a higher average excess return (105 bp) versus Wells Fargo's pair (1.26, 91 bp). Now it's the way we want it: a positive mean/beta relationship. The same is true when looking at average excess returns on days when the market is negative.[21] Alphas do change, but they don't do so dramatically – certainly not enough to restore the original anomalous mean/beta relationship.

---

[21] Of course, "the way we want it" with average excess returns when the market's negative is a negative mean/beta relationship – a negatively sloped line in the 4th quadrant.

To see this in a more general way, note that α_i can be partitioned (as mentioned above) into a part related to days when the market is negative, α_i^-, and when it is positive, α_i^+: [22]

Since $\bar{r}_i = \lambda \bar{r}_i^- + (1-\lambda)\bar{r}_i^+$, $\quad \bar{r}_m = \lambda \bar{r}_m^- + (1-\lambda)\bar{r}_m^+$ and $\quad \bar{r}_i = \beta_i \bar{r}_m + \alpha_i$, then

$$\lambda \bar{r}_i^- + (1-\lambda)\bar{r}_i^+ = \beta_i\big(\lambda \bar{r}_m^- + (1-\lambda)\bar{r}_m^+\big) + \alpha_i.$$

or,
$$\alpha_i = \lambda(\bar{r}_i^- - \beta_i \bar{r}_m^-) + (1-\lambda)(\bar{r}_i^+ - \beta_i \bar{r}_m^+)$$

or,
$$\alpha_i = \lambda \alpha_i^- + (1-\lambda)\alpha_i^+$$

What's true for each individual stock is also true for the average alpha across all stocks. By itself, though, the average alpha is not too interesting. It's equal to the average over all the 90 stock average excess returns minus the average beta times the average CRSP excess return:

$$\bar{\alpha} = \bar{\bar{r}} - \bar{\beta}\,\bar{r}_{CRSP}$$

Thus if the two returns are equal and the average beta is one, the average alpha is zero. But even if zero or close to zero how it gets partitioned and the variation within the total and the partitions themselves is worth looking at. For the 90 stocks the total average alpha and its two partitions (expressed in basis points, standard deviations in parenthesis) are:

$$\overline{\alpha_i} = \lambda\,\overline{\alpha_i^-} + (1-\lambda)\,\overline{\alpha_i^+}$$
$$2.4 = \lambda\,2.7 + (1-\lambda)2.2$$
$$(1.6) \quad\quad (4.4) \quad\quad\quad (5.0)$$

Although there is somewhat more variation, notice that the total average alpha of 2.4 bp more or less survives in the two partitions.[23] This needn't have been the case. It's perfectly possible, for example, that there be a positive alpha on days when the market's negative and a negative alpha on positive days (as was the case in the two stock example above) or the other way around. It's also possible for these alphas to be large. But it's difficult to supply a reason why this would happen. If other factors of return are embedded in alphas, then they should be operational whether the market is up or down. If they weren't then they'd be incorporated into beta. Alphas that remain more or less the same as the absolute value of returns get bigger means that alpha has much less of a chance to influence average excess returns as we move away from around the middle of the distribution.

When expected excess returns are estimated with **PAN AERs** alphas get considerably smaller as pointed out in footnote 23 and their diminished influence is manifestly evident.

---

[22] Here I am taking advantage of the fact that beta has been calculated over all days (positive and negative).

[23] The positive and negative alphas here are based on the large negative and positive average returns for the 90 stocks over the 24 year period (-73.9bp and 73.3bp respectively) not the scaled down relative negative and positive excess returns that go into the calculation of **PAN AERs**. If alphas are calculated using **PAN AERs** (*i.e.*, $\alpha_i =$ **PAN AER**$_i - \beta_i\,\bar{r}_{CRSP}$) and partitioned into positive and negative parts and then averaged, the two parts have the same average as the total ($\bar{\alpha} = (1-\bar{\beta})\,\bar{r}_{CRSP} = .17\,bp$) and are all very small. The standard deviations are .184 bp, for total alpha, .180 bp for the negative partition alpha and .210 bp for the positive partition alpha.

But why the dramatic increase in R²s when we look at **PAN AERs** versus just regular **AERs**? To get an appreciation of how this happens we need to go back to equation (5), which for reference is repeated here:

$$R^2_{\beta,\bar{r}} = 1 \div \left[1 + \left(\frac{1}{\bar{r}_m^2}\right)\left(\frac{\hat{\sigma}_\alpha^2}{\hat{\sigma}_\beta^2}\right)\right],$$

and plug in some actual historic values for the full 24-year period:

								R² with	
	$\bar{r}_m$	$\bar{r}_m^2$	$\frac{1}{\bar{r}_m^2}$	σ_α^2	σ_β^2	$\frac{\sigma_\alpha^2}{\sigma_\beta^2}$	$\left(\frac{1}{\bar{r}_m^2}\right)\left(\frac{\sigma_\alpha^2}{\sigma_\beta^2}\right)$	$\sigma_{\alpha,\beta}=0$	$\sigma_{\alpha,\beta}\neq 0$
	(A)	(B)	(C)	(D)	(E)	(F)	(G)		
Overall	3.2	10	.09877	2.6	.084	31	3.034	.25	.23
When Market is									
Positive	75.2	5656	.00018	24.6	.084	294	.052	.95	.95
Negative	-81.0	6558	.00015	19.3	.084	231	.035	.97	.97

Column (A) is the average daily excess return in basis points (bp) for the CRSP Index
Column (D) is the variance of alpha in bp²

The main driver in creating a high $R^2_{\beta,\bar{r}}$ is the size of the mean daily excess returns when the market (*i.e.,* the CRSP Index) is positive (75.2 bp) and when it is negative (-81.0 bp). Because they are large, when they are squared (column (B)) and divided into 1, the result is a very small number (column (C)). So it really doesn't matter what the ratio of the two variances in column (F) is, even though that ratio gets larger due to the increased variability of the partitioned alpha in the tails of the distribution. The reciprocal of the square of the mean daily excess return (column C) dominates the final calculation. When the market is either positive or negative it's about .0002. With the regular **AERs** it is .1 (500 times larger). Carry this through to column (G) and it's easy to account for the huge differences in $R^2_{\beta,\bar{r}}$ s

Finally, for **AERs** (the first row in Table B 1) it doesn't seem to matter much over the entire 24 year period (whereas it did over the twelve 2-year sub-periods, see page 12) to the size of $R^2_{\beta,\bar{r}}$ s if the covariance of alpha and beta ($\sigma_{\alpha,\beta}$) is zero (.25) or different from zero (.23).

Appendix C

		Regression with all the data		Alt. Beta		Esitmated Annualized Expected Excess Returns (%)			Capitlization As of 12/31/10
		R^2	β	(1% out)	β Diff	AER	PAN AER	Diff	($ Billion)
1	Exxon Mobil Corporation	.35	.77	.71	.06	10	11	-1	368.7
2	Apple Inc.	.21	1.15	1.24	-.09	25	18	7	295.9
3	Microsoft Corporation	.40	1.11	1.14	-.03	17	17	-1	238.8
4	General Electric Company	**.53**	1.14	1.11	.04	11	16	-6	194.9
5	Wal-Mart Stores Inc	.25	.72	.75	-.03	9	11	-2	192.1
6	Chevron Corporation	.34	.80	.73	.07	11	11		183.6
7	IBM Corp.	.33	.90	.92	-.02	11	13	-3	182.3
8	The Procter & Gamble Company	.19	.54	.54	.00	10	8	1	180.1
9	AT&T, Inc.	.27	.75	.72	.03	9	10	-2	173.6
10	Johnson & Johnson	.23	.56	.54	.02	11	8	2	169.9
11	JPMorgan Chase & Co.	.51	1.51	1.44	.07	15	20	-6	165.8
12	Wells Fargo & Company	.39	1.26	1.17	.09	17	17	-1	162.7
13	Oracle Corporation	.30	1.37	1.46	-.09	28	21	6	158.1
14	The Coca-Cola Company	.21	.56	.56	.00	8	8	-1	152.7
15	Pfizer Inc.	.27	.78	.80	-.02	11	11	-1	140.3
16	Citigroup Inc	.43	**1.71**	**1.54**	**.16**	12	**22**	**-11**	137.4
17	Bank of America Corporation	.41	1.53	1.37	.16	11	20	-10	134.5
18	Intel Corporation	.39	1.32	1.40	-.08	19	20	-2	117.3
19	Schlumberger Limited	.30	1.05	.99	.06	12	14	-3	113.9
20	Merck & Co. Inc.	.23	.74	.73	.02	8	10	-3	111.0
21	Pepsico, Inc.	.17	.53	.51	.02	10	8	1	103.5
22	Verizon Communications Inc.	.25	.70	.68	.02	9	10	-1	101.1
23	ConocoPhillips	.28	.84	.78	.06	11	12	-1	100.1
24	HP Inc.	.31	1.17	1.25	-.08	12	18	-6	92.2
25	McDonald's Corp.	.20	.59	.60	-.01	12	9	2	81.1
26	Occidental Petroleum Corporation	.30	.94	.82	.13	14	12	1	79.7
27	Abbott Laboratories	.19	.61	.65	-.04	10	10		74.1
28	United Technologies Corporation	.42	.94	.92	.02	14	13	1	72.7
29	Disney Company	.39	1.05	1.02	.03	12	15	-4	71.0
30	3M Company	.36	.77	.76	.00	11	11		61.7
31	Caterpillar Inc.	.38	1.09	1.10	-.01	14	16	-2	59.4
32	The Home Depot, Inc.	.38	1.07	1.08	-.01	16	16	-1	57.5
33	Ford Motor Co.	.28	1.16	1.16	-.01	10	17	-7	57.1
34	Amgen Inc.	.22	.90	.96	-.06	17	13	3	51.9
35	U.S. Bancorp	.38	1.14	1.09	.05	14	16	-3	51.7
36	American Express Company	.50	1.37	1.28	.09	15	18	-3	51.7
37	Altria Group, Inc.	.12	.51	.53	-.02	16	8	7	51.4
38	The Boeing Company	.31	.92	.90	.02	11	13	-2	47.9
39	CVS Health Corporation	.19	.72	.72	.00	13	11	1	47.2
40	EMC Corporation	.30	1.42	1.50	-.09	27	22	5	47.2
41	Union Pacific Corporation	.32	.86	.87	-.02	13	13	-1	45.7
42	Comcast Corporation	.30	1.12	1.11	.01	17	16		45.7
43	E. I. du Pont de Nemours	.38	.96	.95	.02	9	14	-6	45.5
44	Bristol-Myers Squibb Company	.23	.72	.77	-.05	11	11		45.3
45	Apache Corp.	.21	.95	.87	.08	14	13		43.5
46	Emerson Electric Co.	.45	.99	.97	.02	10	14	-5	43.0
47	Target Corp.	.32	1.01	.95	.06	15	14		42.6
48	Honeywell International Inc.	.40	1.09	1.08	.01	13	15	-3	41.5
49	Eli Lilly and Company	.22	.73	.72	.01	11	11		40.4
50	Medtronic plc	.22	.75	.76	-.02	14	11	3	39.8
51	UnitedHealth Group Incorporated	.17	.82	.72	.10	21	12	9	39.7
52	The Dow Chemical Company	.36	1.07	1.06	.01	10	15	-5	39.6
53	Colgate-Palmolive Co.	.19	.56	.57	-.01	12	9	3	38.8
54	Texas Instruments Inc.	.33	**1.34**	**1.50**	**-.16**	21	22	-1	38.2
55	Anadarko Petroleum Corporation	.23	1.03	.94	.09	14	14		37.7

Appendix C -- continued

		Regression with all the data		Alt. Beta		Esitmated Annualized Expected Excess Returns (%)			Capitlization As of 12/31/10
		R^2	β	β (1% out)	β Diff	AER	PAN AER	Diff	($ Biilion)
56	The Bank of New York Mellon Corp.	.47	1.39	1.27	.12	15	19	-4	37.5
57	Halliburton Company	.24	1.17	1.07	.09	16	16	-1	37.1
58	Walgreens Boots Alliance, Inc.	.23	.75	.76	-.01	15	12	3	35.9
59	Deere & Company	.32	1.02	.99	.03	15	15		35.1
60	Lowe's Companies, Inc	.32	1.08	1.10	-.02	21	16	5	34.6
61	Devon Energy Corporation	.20	.92	.86	.06	13	13		33.9
62	NIKE, Inc.	.22	.84	.83	.01	18	12	5	33.2
63	Southern Company	.13	.38	.37	.01	11	6	4	32.1
64	The PNC Financial Services Group	.39	1.21	1.15	.06	12	17	-5	31.9
65	Danaher Corp.	.38	.88	.89	.00	18	13	5	30.8
66	Corning Inc	.27	1.35	1.42	-.07	13	20	-7	30.2
67	Newmont Mining Corporation	**.02**	**.32**	**.22**	.11	**7**	**4**	3	29.9
68	Baxter International Inc.	.17	.61	.64	-.03	11	9	1	29.5
69	FedEx Corporation	.32	.98	1.02	-.03	14	14		29.3
70	Carnival Corporation	.34	1.14	1.11	.03	14	16	-3	28.0
71	Celgene Corporation	.14	1.14	1.18	-.04	**35**	16	**18**	27.8
72	Exelon Corporation	.17	.57	.51	.07	9	8	1	27.5
73	General Dynamics Corporation	.25	.70	.74	-.05	17	10	6	26.8
74	Aflac Incorporated	.33	1.15	1.02	.13	18	14	3	26.6
75	Illinois Tool Works Inc.	.42	.94	.94	.00	13	14	-1	26.5
76	Johnson Controls Inc	.38	1.04	1.05	.00	15	15	-1	25.9
77	Hess Corporation	.28	1.02	.92	.11	11	14	-4	25.8
78	Kimberly-Clark Corporation	.17	.51	.53	-.02	9	8	1	25.7
79	The Travelers Companies, Inc.	.35	.93	.85	.09	12	12	-1	25.6
80	Franklin Resources, Inc	.50	1.39	1.36	.03	16	19	-4	25.4
81	Dominion Resources, Inc.	.21	.49	.46	.03	10	7	2	25.2
82	Baker Hughes Incorporated	.22	1.06	.99	.07	10	15	-5	24.7
83	CSX Corp.	.34	1.01	1.04	-.03	11	15	-5	24.2
84	Duke Energy Corporation	.16	.51	.47	.03	9	7	1	23.6
85	State Street Corporation	.41	1.42	1.29	.13	15	18	-4	23.3
86	Norfolk Southern Corporation	.33	.98	1.01	-.02	10	15	-5	22.8
87	Automatic Data Processing, Inc	.37	.81	.84	-.03	12	12	-1	22.8
88	General Mills, Inc.	.15	.39	.40	.00	8	6	1	22.6
89	Thermo Fisher Scientific, Inc.	.32	.93	.93	.00	13	13	-1	22.0
90	Cummins Inc.	.37	1.30	1.26	.05	17	18	-1	21.8
	Average	.30	.95	.93	.02	14	14	-1	72.74
	sd	.10	.29	.29	.06	5	4	4	66.2
	Max	.53	1.71	1.54	.16	35	22	18	368.7
	Min	.02	.32	.22	-.16	7	4	-11	21.8

Note: in each column maximums and minimums are in **bold.**

References

Banz, R. (1981). The Relationship Between Return and Market Value of Common Stocks. *Journal of Financial Economics*, pp. 3-18.

Black, Fischer, Michael C. Jensen and Myron Scholes. (1972). "The Capital Asset Pricing Model: Some Empirical Tests,". (M. C. Jensen, Ed.) *Studies in the Theory of Capital Markets.* , 79-121.

Black, Fischer. (1972). "Capital Market Equilibrium with Restricted Borrowing.". *Journal of Business*, 444-454.

Brière, Marie, Valérie Mignon, Kim Oosterlinck and Ariane Szafarz. (2015). Is the Market Portfolio Efficient? A New Test to Revisit Roll (1977) versus Levy and Roll (2010) Controversy. *EconomiX Working Papers, University of Paris West - Nanterre la Défense, EconomiX.*

Campbell, John Y., Lo, Andrew, MacKinlay, Craig A. (1997). *The Econometrics of Financial Markets.* Princeton, NJ: Princeton University Press.

Elton, Edwin J. (1999). "Presidential Address: Expected Return, Realized Return and Asset Pricing Tests". *Journal of Finance*, 1199-1220.

Elton, Edwin J., Martin J. Gruber, Stephen J. Brown, William N. Goetzmann. January 2014, ©2014. Modern Portfolio Theory and Investment Analysis, 9th Edition. (2014). *Modern Portfolio Theory and Investment Analysis, 9th Edition.* New York: John Wiley and Sons.

Fama, E. F. (1963). Mandelbrot and the Stable Paretian Hypothesis. *The Journal of Business*, pp. 420-429.

Fama, Eugene F. and French, Kenneth R. (1993). "Common Risk Factors in the Returns on Stocks and Bonds". . *Journal of Financial Economics*, 3-56.

Fama, Eugene F. and French, Kenneth R. (2015). A Five-Factor Asset Pricing Model. *Journal of Financial Economics*, 1-22.

Fama, Eugene F. and French, Kenneth R. (Summer 2004). "The Capital Asset Pricing Model: Theory and Evidence.". *Journal of Economic Perspectives*, 25-46.

Fama, Eugene F. and James D. MacBeth. (1973). Risk, Return and Equilibrium: Empirical Tests. *Journal of Political Economy*, 607-636.

French, K. R. ((2016)). Data Library. http://mba.tuck.dartmouth.edu/pages/faculty/ken.french/data_library.html.

Gibbons, Michael R., Stephen A. Ross and Jay Shanken. (1989). "A Test of the Efficiency of a Given Portfolio.". *Econometrica*, 1121-1152.

Grauer, R. R. (1999). On the Cross-Sectional Relation betweem Returns, Betas, and Size. *The Journal of Finance*, 773-789.

Levy, Moshe and Ritov Ya'acov. (2011, October). Mean-variance efficient portfolios with many assets: 50% short. *Quantitative Finance*, pp. 1461-1471.

Levy, Moshe and Roll, Richard. (2010). The Market Portfolio May Be Mean/Variance Efficient After All. *Review of Financial Studies*, pp. 2464-2491.

Lintner, John. (1965). "The Valuation of Risk Assets and the Selection of Risky Investments in Stock Portfolios and Capital Budgets.". *Review of Economics and Statistics.*, 13-67.

Markowitz, H. M. (1952). Portfolio Selection. *Journal of Finance*, 77-91.

Mossin, J. (1966). Equilibrium in a Capital Asset Market. *Econometrica*, 768-783.

Pettengill, Glenn Chang, George, Hueng, James. (2012). Risk-return Predictions with the Fama-French Three-factor Model Betas. *International Journal of Economics and Finance*, 34-47.

Quine, W. V. (1959). *Methods of Logic.* New York: Henry Holt and Company, Inc.

Roll, Richard. (1977). "A Critique of the Asset Pricing Theory's Tests". *Journal of Financial Economics.*, 129-176.

Roll, Richard and Ross, Stephen A. (1994). On the Cross-sectional Relation between Expected Returns and Betas. *The Journal of Finance*, pp. 101-121.

Rosenberg, Barr, Kenneth Reid, and Ronald Lanstein. (1985). Persuasive evidence of market inefficiency. *Journal of Portfolio Management*, 9-17.

Ross, S. (1976). The arbitrage theory of capital asset pricing. *Journal of Economic Theory.*, pp. 341-360.

Samuelson, P. A. (n.d.). Economic Theory and Wages. In D. M. Wright, *The Impact of the Union* (pp. 312-42). Freeport, NY: Books for Liberty Press.

Sharpe, William. (1964). "Capital Asset Prices: A Theory of Market Equilibrium under Conditions of Risk". *Journal of Finance.*, 425-442.

Tobin, J. (1958). Liquidity Preference as Behavior Towards Risk. *Review of Economic Studies*, 65-86.

Treynor, J. L. (1962). Toward a Theory of Market Value of Risky Assets. *Available at SSRN: http://ssrn.com/abstract=628187 or http://dx.doi.org/10.2139/ssrn.628187.*

Yahoo-Finance-Website. (n.d.). https://au.finance.yahoo.com/q/hp?s=YHOO.

www.ingramcontent.com/pod-product-compliance
Lightning Source LLC
Chambersburg PA
CBHW081312180526
45170CB00007B/2678